Snowdonia &
North Wales

Rebecca Ford

Credits

Footprint credits
Editor: Nicola Gibbs
Production and layout: Emma Bryers
Maps: Kevin Feeney
Cover: Pepi Bluck

Publisher: Patrick Dawson
Managing Editor: Felicity Laughton
Advertising: Elizabeth Taylor
Sales and marketing: Kirsty Holmes

Photography credits
Front cover: Richard0/Dreamstime.com
Back cover: Len Green/Dreamstime.com

Printed in Great Britain by CPI Antony Rowe,
Chippenham, Wiltshire

MIX
Paper from
responsible sources
FSC® C013604
www.fsc.org

Every effort has been made to ensure that
the facts in this guidebook are accurate.
However, travellers should still obtain advice
from consulates, airlines, etc, about travel
and visa requirements before travelling.
The authors and publishers cannot accept
responsibility for any loss, injury or
inconvenience however caused.

Publishing information
Footprint *Focus Snowdonia & North Wales*
1st edition
© Footprint Handbooks Ltd
May 2013

ISBN: 978 1 909268 26 5
CIP DATA: A catalogue record for this book
is available from the British Library

® Footprint Handbooks and the Footprint
mark are a registered trademark of
Footprint Handbooks Ltd

Published by Footprint
6 Riverside Court
Lower Bristol Road
Bath BA2 3DZ, UK
T +44 (0)1225 469141
F +44 (0)1225 469461
footprinttravelguides.com

Distributed in the USA by Globe Pequot
Press, Guilford, Connecticut

The content of Footprint *Focus Snowdonia
& North Wales* has been taken directly from
Footprint's *Wales Handbook*, which was
researched and written by Rebecca Ford.

Contents

North Wales is perhaps the most Welsh part of Wales. It was to this area that the ancient Britons retreated following the Roman invasion – the Druids had their last stand in Anglesey – and it still retains a distinctive individualism. It's the part of Wales that feels most culturally different to the rest of Britain. Large numbers of people here speak Welsh as their first language and you will certainly hear it spoken on the streets and in the shops.

North Wales is not noted for its sun, but it does have some striking scenery. Its greatest attraction are the hills and mountains of the Snowdonia National Park, which draw thousands of walkers, climbers and mountain bikers each year. Snowdon, the heart of the area, is the highest peak in Britain outside Scotland. Dotted through the national park are towns and villages such as busy Betws-y-Coed, which teems with visitors in walking boots and waterproofs, and delightful Beddgelert, one of the most picturesque towns in Wales.

If you're not an outdoor type you can still find things to do here. The north coast is notorious for its raucous 'kiss me quick' strip of caravans and amusement arcades, but it does contain one jewel in Llandudno, a Victorian resort that still has plenty of traditional charm. Go west and you can explore great castles like Caernarfon, neolithic stones on the pastoral isle of Anglesey, and the fantasy village of Portmeirion.

The southern part of the Snowdonia National Park is in Mid Wales, the place to come if you really want to escape the crowds. The area encompasses a variety of landscapes including Cadair Idris and its surrounding peaks, which provide wild and challenging walking.

There are wildlife-watching opportunities along the coast, where plenty of operators run boat trips that give you the chance to see dolphins, porpoises and seabirds. It's along this stretch of coastline that you'll find places like Harlech, famed for its well-preserved castle, and Aberystwyth, famed for its university.

Planning your trip

Best time to visit Snowdonia and North Wales

The high season runs from April until October, when most attractions are open and summer festivities are organized in almost every town and village. Summer evenings are long, while in winter it can get dark as early as 1600. School holidays (most of July and August) are the busiest time of year, when the most popular tourist destinations, such as the coast and the summit of Snowdon itself, can get pretty packed. The best accommodation anywhere in the countryside must be booked well in advance for the summer months. That said, many of Wales' seaside hotspots are also best appreciated once the weather's turned nasty or even in clear winter sunlight.

Climate
The Welsh temperate climate is notoriously unpredictable. Bright, sunny mornings can turn into a downpour in the time it takes to butter your toast. Very generally, the mountains receive more rain than the coast and October to January are the wettest months. Winters can be pretty harsh, especially in the mountains, making hiking conditions treacherous. May to September are the warmest months (in particular July and August), but you can expect rain at any time of the year, even in high summer. So, you'll need to come prepared, and remember the old hikers' adage that there's no such thing as bad weather, only inadequate clothing.

Getting to Snowdonia and North Wales

Air
Cardiff has an international airport (see page 7) with flights from Scotland, Ireland and Europe. There are also daily flights from Amsterdam, from where it is possible to connect with airports all over the world. Otherwise, the main point of entry will be one of the English airports. Competition means it is usually cheapest to fly to one of London's five airports. Flights from North America arrive at Heathrow or Gatwick. Low-cost airlines generally fly into Gatwick, Stansted or Luton. Direct flights from Europe also arrive at Birmingham, Bristol, Liverpool and Manchester airports. Bristol Airport is most convenient for South Wales; Birmingham or Manchester airports are good for Mid and North Wales.

Flights from the rest of the UK and Ireland A small number of budget airlines fly daily to Cardiff International Airport from several British and Irish destinations. Prices on these flights can vary considerably, depending on the time and day of travel and how early you book your ticket. **Eastern Airways** ⓘ *www.easternairways.com*, flies direct from Birmingham, Newcastle and Aberdeen. **Flybe** ⓘ *www.flybe.com*, flies direct from Edinburgh, Glasgow and Belfast. **Aer Lingus** ⓘ *www.aerlingus.com*, flies direct from Dublin. Check the websites regularly to get the best deals.

Flights from continental Europe In addition to regular flights operated by the major national carriers, the surge in budget airline routes means that you can fly from practically anywhere in Europe to somewhere in Britain at cheap rates. Fares for a return ticket range

Don't miss...

from €15 to €300 on a scheduled flight. Budget airlines offer no frills: no meals, no reserved seating and baggage restrictions.

If you are flying direct to Cardiff, **Flybe** ① *www.flybe.com*, flies from Paris; **Vuelling Airlines** ① *www.vueling.com*, flies from Barcelona, Malaga and Alicante; **Thomson** ① *www.thomson.co.uk*, flies from Faro; **KLM** ① *www.klm.com*, flies from Amsterdam; and **Lufthansa** ① *www.lufthansa.com*, flies from Dusseldorf.

Flights from North America There are no direct flights to Cardiff from North America, but journeys can be made via Amsterdam, from where there are frequent onward connections to Cardiff, taking just one hour 25 minutes. Alternatively, there are regular non-stop flights to London from many US and Canadian cities, including Atlanta, Boston, Calgary, Chicago, Dallas, Denver, Houston, Las Vegas, Los Angeles, Miami, Montreal, New York, Philadelphia, Phoenix, San Francisco, Seattle, Toronto, Vancouver and Washington DC, and many more connections to other cities. Non-stop flights are also available from New York to Manchester and Birmingham.

Flights from Australia and New Zealand There are no direct flights to Cardiff from Australia or New Zealand. The cheapest scheduled flights to London are via Asia with **Gulf Air** ① *www.gulfair.com*, **Royal Brunei** ① *www.bruneiair.com*, or **Thai Airways** ① *www.thaiair.com*. Flights via Africa or North America are more expensive. The cheapest scheduled flights from New Zealand are with **Korean Air** ① *www.koreanair.com*, **Thai Airways**, or JAL ① *www.jal.com*, all of which fly via their home cities. The most direct route is via North America with **United Airlines** ① *www.ual.com*, via Chicago or Los Angeles. **Emirates** ① *www.emirates.com*, flies to Birmingham and Manchester from Sydney via Dubai, and Manchester is also served via Singapore on **Singapore Airlines** ① *www.singaporeair.com*. Prices are slightly higher than flights to London.

Airport information
Arriving in Cardiff Cardiff International Airport (CWL) ① *Rhoose, near Barry, T01446-711111, www.cwlfly.com*, Wales' small international airport, is 12 miles southwest of Cardiff's city centre and around a 30- to 40-minute taxi journey. The terminal's facilities include a few small bars selling drinks, snacks and teas and coffees, newsagents, a selection of duty free shops, and a children's play area. The airport is easily reached by car via the A4055, or taking the A4225 from the A48 or junction 33 off the M4. The taxi office is in the Arrivals hall and taxis can be prebooked on T01446-711747, approximately £25-30 to

the city centre. Air buses operate regularly between the city's central train and main bus station and the airport, costing approximately £3.90.

Arriving in London National Express operates a frequent service between London's main airports. **London Heathrow Airport** ⓘ *16 miles west of London between junctions 3 and 4 on the M4, T0844-335 1801, www.heathrowairport.com*, is one of the world's busiest international airports and it has five terminals, so when leaving London, it's important to check which terminal to go to before setting out for the airport. To get into central London, the cheapest option is the London Underground Piccadilly Line (50 minutes). The fastest option is **Heathrow Express** ⓘ *T0845-6001515, www.heathrowexpress.com*, taking 15-20 minutes. There is a train service, **Heathrow Connect** ⓘ *Heathrow, T0845-748 4950, www.heathrowconnect.com*, which takes 25 minutes. Coaches to destinations all over the country are run by **National Express** ⓘ *www.nationalexpress.com*. There are also buses to Reading for trains to Bristol and southwest England (www.railair.com).

London Gatwick Airport ⓘ *28 miles south of London, off junction 9 on the M23, T0844-892 03222, www.gatwickairport.com*, has two terminals, North and South, with all the usual facilities. To central London, there is the **Gatwick Express** ⓘ *T0845-850 1530, www.gatwickexpress.com, from £17.75 single online*, which takes 30 minutes. **Thameslink** rail services run from King's Cross, Farringdon, Blackfriars and London Bridge stations. Contact **National Rail Enquiries** ⓘ *T0845-748 4950, www.nationalrail.co.uk*, for further information. **easyBus** ⓘ *www.easybus.co.uk*, is the cheapest option, with prices at £9.99 single, taking just over an hour. A taxi takes a similar time and costs from around £60.

London City Airport ⓘ *Royal Dock, 6 miles (15 mins' drive) east of the City of London, T020-7646 0000, www.londoncityairport.com*. Take the **Docklands Light Railway** (DLR) to Canning Town (seven minutes) for the **Jubilee line** or a connecting shuttle bus service. A taxi into central London will cost around £35.

London Luton Airport ⓘ *30 miles north of central London, 2 miles off the M1 at junction 10, southeast of Luton, Beds, T01582-405100, www.london-luton.co.uk*. Regular **First Capital Connect** trains run to central London; a free shuttle bus service operates between the airport terminal and the station. **Green Line** ⓘ *www.greenline.co.uk*, coaches run to central London, as does **easyBus** ⓘ *www.easybus.co.uk*. **National Express** ⓘ *www.nationalexpress.com*, operates coaches to many destinations. A taxi takes 50 minutes, costing from £70.

Stansted Airport ⓘ *35 miles northeast of London (near Cambridge) by junction 8 of the M11, T0844-335 1803, www.stanstedairport.com*. **Stansted Express** ⓘ *T0845-600 7245, www.stanstedexpress.com*, runs trains to London's Liverpool Street Station (45 minutes, £22.50 single). **easyBus** ⓘ *www.easybus.co.uk, from £2*, **Terravision** ⓘ *www.terravision.eu, £9*, and **National Express** ⓘ *www.nationalexpress.com, from £8.50*, run to central London (55 minutes to East London, one hour 30 minutes to Victoria). A taxi to central London takes around an hour to one hour 30 minutes, depending on traffic, and costs around £99.

Arriving at other UK airports Bristol International Airport (BRS) ⓘ *T0870-121 2747, www.bristolairport.co.uk*, eight miles south of the city centre, on the A38, has one terminal with standard facilities. A taxi to Bristol city centre costs £22, or the **Bristol International Flyer** coach links the airport with the railway station (Temple Meads) and the central bus station for onward connections, £11 return, 30 minutes.

Birmingham International Airport (BHX) ⓘ *T0121-767 5511, www.bhx.co.uk*, eight miles east of the city centre, has two terminals with standard facilities. A taxi to the centre costs around £25, or frequent trains run the 10-minute journey into the city centre. Connections to Wales can be made by rail or coach, with **National Express** ① *www.nationalexpress.com*.

Liverpool John Lennon Airport (LPL) ① *T0870-750 8484, www.liverpooljohn lennonairport.com*, is seven miles southeast of the city in Speke. A regular bus runs to Liverpool city centre, from where connecting buses and trains can be taken.

Manchester International Airport (MAN) ① *T0161-489 3000, www.manchesterairport. co.uk*, south of the city centre, at Junction 5 of the M56. There are three terminals. Trains run from Manchester Piccadilly to North Wales. **National Express** ① *www.nationalexpress.com*, runs from Terminals 1 and 2. A taxi into the city centre should cost around £20.

Newcastle International Airport (NCL) ① *T0870-122 1488, www.newcastleairport.com*, is five miles north of the city. Metro trains run from the airport between 0545 and 2305, every 10 minutes, taking 20 minutes to the city centre or the central train station; single fare £2.10. **National Express** ① *www.nationalexpress.com*, coaches also run from the airport.

Rail

There are fast and frequent rail services to Cardiff from London, Bristol, Birmingham and most other major cities. From London, trains leave from Paddington station for South Wales or from Euston station for Mid or North Wales. Trains from Birmingham, Manchester and London also head to Mid Wales (Machynlleth, Llandudno or Welshpool) and North Wales (Holyhead, Bangor, Llandudno, Porthmadog and Pwllheli); it may be necessary to change more than once. Ticket pricing is complicated (see page 11), but to get the best deal you should book in advance. Note that travel on Fridays or during the rush hour (before 1000 weekdays) is generally more expensive.

From continental Europe All international train connections pass through London. **Eurostar** ① *T0990-186186, www.eurostar.com*, operates high-speed trains to London Waterloo from Paris (three hours) and Brussels (two hours 40 minutes) via Lille (two hours). There are substantial discounts for children (4-11 years) and for passengers who are under 26 years on the day of travel. It is worth keeping an eye open for special offers, especially in the low season. All other rail connections will involve some kind of ferry crossing (see below). For full details on rail services, contact your national railway or **Rail Europe**, www.raileurope.com; they also provide information on routes, timetables, fares and discount passes.

Road

Bus/coach Road links to Wales are good and this is the cheapest form of travel. The main operator between England and Wales is **National Express** ① *T08705-808080, www. nationalexpress.com*. Buses from London leave from Victoria station and travel via Bristol to South Wales (Newport, Cardiff, Swansea, Carmarthen and Pembroke Dock); via Birmingham and Shrewsbury to Mid Wales (Welshpool, Aberystwyth) or via Chester to North Wales (Wrexham, Llandudno, Bangor, Pwllheli and Holyhead). From the north of England, buses travel via Birmingham to South Wales, or via Manchester or Liverpool to North Wales, from where onward connections can be made. Tickets can be bought at bus stations or from a number of agents throughout the country. It's also worth checking **www.megabus.com** for cheaper, but slower, transport from London to Cardiff and Swansea.

Car The most direct way to reach South Wales by car from London and southern and western England is on the **M4** motorway. The M4 crosses the Severn Estuary via the dramatic Severn Bridge (£6.20 per car, toll payable westbound only – you can leave Wales for free!). To North Wales, the **A55** expressway runs all the way from Chester to Holyhead following the coast; or from the Midlands, the **A5** through Llangollen. Mid Wales is best reached by the **A495** from Shrewsbury to Welshpool and then the **A458**; or the **A456** from Birmingham.

    From continental Europe If you're driving from continental Europe you can take the **Eurotunnel Shuttle Service** ① *T0800-969992, www.eurotunnel.com*, a freight train which runs 24 hours a day, 365 days a year, and takes you and your car from Calais to Folkestone in 35-45 minutes. For bookings, call T08705-353535. Foot passengers cannot cross on the Shuttle. You can also take a cross-channel ferry, see below.

Sea

From Ireland There are direct ferry crossings from Ireland to Holyhead in North Wales and to Swansea, Fishguard and Pembroke Dock in the south. There are at least two sailings daily, apart from to Swansea which is served four times a week. There are more frequent sailings during summer. Fares vary considerably depending on the time of day, week and season. Check the websites for promotional offers; discounts are usually available for students and Hostelling International (HI) members.

    Irish Ferries ① *T0818-300400, www.irishferries.com*, runs ferries from Dublin to Holyhead (five daily, three hours 15 minutes) and Rosslare to Pembroke (two daily, three hours 45 minutes). Fast boats are also available.

    Stena Line ① *T01-204 7777 (Ireland), T08447-707070 (UK), www.stenaline.ie*, runs ferries from Dun Laoghaire and Dublin to Holyhead (two daily, one hour 45 minutes) and from Rosslare to Fishguard (two daily, 3½ hours).

From continental Europe There are ferries to England from many European ports; the most useful for access to Wales are **Harwich** (served by boats from Denmark, Germany and the Netherlands); **Dover** (served by boats from Belgium and France); and **Portsmouth** (served by boats from France and Spain). **Poole**, **Portsmouth** and **Plymouth** are also served by boats from France. Prices vary enormously according to season, check prices for specific dates on one of the many online booking agent websites: **www.cheapferry.com**, **www.ferry-to-france.co.uk**, **www.ferrycrossings-uk.co.uk** or **www.ferrysavers.com**, or by contacting major route operators direct: **P&O Ferries** ① *T08716-642121, www.poferries. com*, run from France, Ireland, Belgium and Holland; and **Brittany Ferries** ① *T0871-244 0744, www.brittany-ferries.com*, run from Spain and western France to Britain's south coast.

Paddle steamers During the summer months, the *Waverley* and the *Balmoral* paddle steamers travel from Penarth, Newport, Swansea and Porthcawl down the Bristol Channel to Ilfracombe in Devon and Minehead in Somerset. A one-way ticket costs around £15. This is a very pleasant and leisurely way to travel, however the cruises are cancelled during bad weather. Further information is available from **Waverley Excursions** ① *T0845-130 4647, www.waverleyexcursions.co.uk*.

Transport in Snowdonia and North Wales

Compared to the rest of Western Europe, public transport in Britain is generally poor and can be expensive. Rail, in particular, can cost an arm and a leg, and is notoriously unreliable. Coach travel is cheaper but much slower. Some areas are poorly served by public transport of any kind, and if you plan to spend much time in rural areas, it may be worth hiring a car, especially if you are travelling as a couple or group. A useful website for all national public transport information is **Traveline** ① *T0871-200 2233, www.traveline.info*.

Rail

The rail network in Wales is less extensive than the bus network and generally a more expensive way to travel. However, there are some wonderfully scenic journeys across the middle of the country and many heritage railways still exist (see box, page 12). Most trains operating within Wales are run by **Arriva Trains Wales** ① *T08456-061660, www.arrivatrainswales.co.uk*.

Enquiries and booking National Rail Enquiries ① *T08457-484950, www. nationalrail.co.uk*, are quick and courteous with information on rail services and fares but not always accurate, so double check. They can't book tickets but will provide you with the relevant telephone number. The website www.thetrainline.co.uk shows prices clearly.

Railcards There are a variety of railcards which give discounts on fares for certain groups. Cards are valid for one year and most are available from main stations. You need two passport photos and proof of age or status. A **Young Person's Railcard** is for those aged 16-25 or full-time students aged 26+ in the UK. It costs £28 for one year and gives a 33% discount on most train tickets and some other services (www.16-25railcard.co.uk). A **Senior Citizen's Railcard** is for those aged over 60, it is the same price and offers the same discounts as a Young Person's Railcard (www.senior-railcard.co.uk). A **Disabled Person's Railcard** costs £20 and gives a 33% discount to a disabled person and one other. Pick up an application form from stations and send it to Disabled Person's Railcard Office, PO Box 11631, Laurencekirk AB30 9AA. It may take up to 10 working days to be delivered, so apply in advance (www.disabledpersons-railcard.co.uk). A **Family & Friends Railcard** costs £28 and gives a 33% discount on most tickets for up to four adults travelling together, and 60% discount for up to four children (www.familyandfriends-railcard.co.uk). It's available to buy online as well as in most stations.

Within Wales, the **Explore Wales Pass** (www.arrivatrainswales.co.uk) allows you to travel on all mainline trains and almost all its buses for a specified period. The pass costs £94/children £47 and allows four days' train and eight days' bus travel within a period of eight consecutive days. The **Explore South Wales** and the **Explore North and Mid Wales** passes each cost £64, child £32.

Road

Bicycle Wales, like the rest of Britain, is less cycle-friendly than some countries, but with plenty of rivers, valleys, mountains, coast and moorland to explore, cycling is a great way to get out and about into the heart of the Welsh countryside. You don't need to go mountain biking off-road to enjoy the peace and quiet of the area; there are plenty of rural backroads, especially unclassified roads and country lanes, which are not numbered but are signposted and marked on OS maps. The only problem with more remote areas is the scarcity of spare parts should something go wrong with your bike.

The rail thing

Wales is a great place for lovers of scenic railway journeys – the country is full of them. The railways were vital to the development of the country's industries in the 19th century and trains, hauled first by horses and then by steam, were used to transport goods such as coal and slate from mines and quarries (often set in inaccessible mountain regions) to ports where they could then be loaded onto ships and exported all over the world. It was in 1804 that the first steam locomotive travelled on iron rails, going along the Merthyr tramroad in south Wales. And the world's first passenger railway service was launched in Wales in 1807, taking people around Swansea Bay. When the industries declined so did the railways – and the final death knell for many were the beeching cuts of the 1960s, which axed lines throughout Britain, badly affecting rural areas of Wales. However, many old railway lines that were abandoned have been carefully restored by volunteers who now run vintage trains (usually steam) along the tracks. The best known scenic routes are in the north, but there are a few in the south of Wales too. Wales also boasts Britain's only mountain railway, which travels up Snowdon.

South Wales
Brecon Mountain Railway, Merthyr Tydfil, www.breconmountainrailway.co.uk.

Mid Wales
Talyllyn Railway, Tywyn, www.talyllyn. co.uk; **Vale of Rheidol Railway**, Aberystwyth, www.rheidolrailway.co.uk; **Welshpool & Llanfair Light Railway**, Llanfair Caereinion, www.wllr.org.uk.

North Wales
Bala Lake Railway, www.bala-lake-railway.co.uk; **Ffestiniog Railway** and **Welsh Highland Railway**, Porthmadog, www.festrail.co.uk; **Llanberis Lake Railway**, www.lake-railway.co.uk.

Information on these services can be found at www.greatlittletrainsof wales.co.uk.

Other scenic railways include: **Fairbourne & Barmouth Steam Railway**, Fairbourne, www.fairbournerailway.com; **Gwili Railway**, near Carmarthen, www.gwili-railway.co.uk; **Llangollen Railway**, www.llangollen-railway.co.uk; **Snowdon Mountain Railway**, Llanberis, www.snowdonrailway.co.uk; and the **Teifi Valley Railway**, Cardigan, www.teifivalleyrailway.org.

There are also forest trails and dedicated routes along canal towpaths and disused railway tracks. These are part of the expanding National Cycle Network, which is covered by the *Official Guide to the National Network* (£9.99), published by the charity **SUSTRANS** ① *T0117-929 0888, www.sustrans.co.uk*. There is also a series of demanding long-distance routes. The Wales Tourist Board provides good information at **www.cycling.visitwales. com**. The **Cyclists' Touring Club** (CTC) ① *T01483-417217, www.ctc.org.uk*, the largest cycling organization in the UK, provides a wide range of services and information on transport, cycle hire and routes, from day rides to longer tours.

Transporting your bicycle You can cut down on the amount of pedalling you have to do by transporting your bike by train. Bikes can be taken free on most local rail services on a first come-first served basis, but only outside morning and evening rush hours (0730-0930 and 1600-1900). On long-distance routes you'll have to make a reservation at least

Pedal power

Wales offers some superb opportunities for cyclists, with everything from gentle circuits for families to challenging mountain bike trails for the adventurous (and fit) biker. You can cycle alongside canal towpaths, down quiet country lanes, beside lakes and reservoirs and along forest and mountain tracks.

The country has three long-distance trails that can be ridden over about a week:

The Lôn Las Cymru National Cycle Route (250 miles) runs north to south and takes you across the Snowdonia National Park and the Cambrian Mountains. It starts in Holyhead, Anglesey and cuts across the country to Cardiff or Chepstow.

The Celtic Trail (220 miles) goes from west to east, starting at Fishguard on the lovely Pembrokeshire coast and going across the country to Chepstow. It follows canal towpaths, disused railway lines and quiet lanes.

The Lôn Cambrian Trail (113 miles) crosses Mid Wales, running between Shrewsbury on the border and Aberystwyth – where it links to the Lôn Teifi route (98 miles) which goes on to Fishguard.

Wales also boasts some of the finest mountain biking in the world. The best-known tracks and bike bases are listed below.

Afan Forest Park, T01639-850564, www.afanforestpark.co.uk, southeast, near Neath, with four trails.

Brecon Beacons National Park, www.mtbbreconbeacons.co.uk, the active heart of Wales with 14 mountain bike routes, suitable for novices and the more experienced.

Coed y Brenin, T01341-440747, in North Wales, near Dolgellau, Wales' best-known mountain biking centre, with good facilities and an expanding network of trails.

Cwmcarn Forest, T01495-272001, www.cwmcarnforest.co.uk, in the southeast corner, half an hour from Cardiff and close to Newport, has the Whyte Twrch Trail.

Gwydyr Forest, www.forestry.gov.uk, in the north near Betws-y-Coed, has a long mountain trail.

Llanwrtyd Wells, Mid Wales, is a good base for exploring on a bike as it offers access to fine, unspoilt countryside and a variety of trails.

Machynlleth, Mid Wales, has three trails that start from the town centre and a purpose-built trail in the nearby Dyfi Forest.

Nant yr Arian, T01970-890453, near Aberystwyth, is set in the remote mountains, it has several trails including the challenging Syfydrin Trail.

These aren't the only places to cycle in the country though – there are cycle paths and trails everywhere. Just ask at local TICs and check out the following websites for loads more information on everything from maps, trail guides, bike repair shops and places to stay: www.mbwales.com for mountain biking; www.visitwales.co.uk for all sorts of cycling info; www.sustrans. org.uk for maps and general information.

24 hours in advance and pay a small charge. Space is limited on trains so it's a good idea to book as far in advance as possible. Bus and coach companies will not usually carry bikes, with the exception of national park bus services, such as the **Snowdon Sherpa**. Details are available on the CTC website.

Rental Bike rental is available at cycle shops in most large towns and cities and tourist centres. Expect to pay from around £20-30 per day, with discounts for longer periods, plus a refundable deposit. There are cycle shops and cycle hire companies in most large towns, and smaller towns and villages in popular tourist areas.

Bus and coach Travelling around Wales by bus is generally the cheapest form of public transport. Roads are well maintained and there are good bus links between towns and cities, but far less frequent in more remote rural areas. While it's possible to travel almost anywhere by bus, it can be slow-going and patience is required. There is a vast network of local and regional services throughout the country, including national parks. When travelling on local buses, try to have the right money as change is not always available.

Reservations Information on services throughout Wales is available from **Traveline Cymru** ① *T0870-608208, www.traveline-cymru.org.uk*. Bus companies include: **Arriva Cymru** ① *T08701-201088, www.arriva.co.uk*, serving north and west Wales; **First Cymru** ① *T01792-582233, www.firstcymru.co.uk*, serving southwest Wales; **National Express** ① *T08705-808080, www.nationalexpress.com*, serving major towns and cities throughout the country; and **Stagecoach** ① *T01633-838856, www.stagecoachbus.com/south_wales*, serving southeast Wales.

A number of travel passes are available. Full-time students, those aged under 25 or over 60 or those registered disabled, can buy a **Coach Card** for £10 which is valid for one year and gets you a 30% discount on all fares. Children normally travel for half price, but with a **Family Card** costing £16, two children travel free with two adults. Available to overseas passport holders, the **Brit Xplorer Pass** offers unlimited travel on all National Express buses. Passes cost from £79 for seven days, £139 for 14 days and £219 for its month-long **Rolling Stone Pass**. They can be bought from major airports and bus terminals.

Car Travelling with your own transport is the ideal way to explore the country. This allows you the freedom to explore remote places in your own time. The main disadvantages are traffic congestion and parking, but this is only a problem in the main cities and on major roads, particularly at weekends and on bank holidays. Roads in Wales are generally a lot less busy than those in England, and driving is relatively stress-free, especially on the B-roads and minor roads.

Motoring organizations can help with route planning, traffic advice, insurance and breakdown cover. The two main ones are: the **Automobile Association (AA)** ① *T0800-085 2721, emergency number T0800-887766, www.theaa.com*, which offers a year's breakdown cover starting at £38, and the **Royal Automobile Club (RAC)** ① *T0844-273 4341, emergency number T08000-828282, www.rac.co.uk*, which has a year's breakdown cover starting at £31.99. Both have cover for emergency assistance. You can still call the emergency numbers if you're not a member, but you'll have to a pay a large fee.

Car hire Car hire is expensive and the minimum you can expect to pay is around £100 per week for a small car. Always check and compare conditions, such as mileage limitations, excess payable in the case of an accident, etc. Small, local hire companies often offer better deals than the larger multinationals. Most companies prefer payment with a credit card – some insist on it – otherwise you'll have to leave a large deposit (£100 or more). You need to have had a full driver's licence for at least a year and to be aged between 21 (25 for some companies) and 70.

Where to stay in Snowdonia and North Wales

Accommodation in Wales is plentiful, and the quality of what's available has improved greatly in recent years. Hotels range from world-class luxury, for which you can expect to pay at least £100 to over £250 a night, to dilapidated concerns with dodgy plumbing and threadbare carpets, though thankfully the latter have almost disappeared. For the privilege of staying at one of these less charming places you can still expect to pay £50-60 a night for a double room. Most of the more salubrious hotels, the ones that can afford to pay the cleaner but may not offer full room service, are likely to cost between £80 and £150 for a double room for a night. Generally it's still true to say that guests paying over £80 a night can expect a decent level of comfort and service: from well-sprung mattresses to fluffy bath towels and flowers in the room.

Hotels

Hotels range from top-notch country houses, with extensive grounds and sometimes spa facilities to smaller establishments like cosy inns. Wales also has an increasing number of boutique hotels which are small, classy and contemporary. You'll also find some restaurants with rooms – where accommodation tends to be good quality but simpler, as the emphasis is on the food – and inns, which are offering increasingly decent rooms.

At the lower end of the scale, there is often little to choose between cheaper hotels and guesthouses or B&Bs – in fact a good B&B can often be far better than a low-grade hotel, offering higher standards of comfort (and often cleanliness) and a more personal service. However, many small hotels are really just guesthouses, and are often family-run and every bit as friendly. Note that some hotels, especially in town centres or in fishing ports, may also be rather noisy, as the bar can often be the social hub. Rooms in most mid-range to expensive hotels almost always have bathrooms en suite. Many upmarket hotels offer excellent room-only deals in the low season. An efficient last-minute booking service is **www.laterooms.com**, which specializes in weekend breaks. Also note that many hotels offer cheaper rates for online booking through agencies such as **www.lastminute. com**. Some of the best accommodation is collected in the brochure by **Welsh Rarebits** ① *T01570-470785, www.rarebits.co.uk.*

Guesthouses

Guesthouses occupy the middle ground between hotels and B&Bs. The quality of accommodation in guesthouses varies wildly: some provide exceptional value for the money in houses of great character; while others have seen much better days. They can usually charge anything from £50-100 for the night, occasionally quoting initially for half-board (dinner, bed and breakfast). Some have a restaurant, which may or may not be open to non-residents.

Guesthouses are often large, converted family homes with five or six rooms. They tend to be slightly more expensive than B&Bs, charging between around £35 and £55 per person per night. Although they are often less personal, they can provide better facilities, such as en suite bathrooms, TV in each room and private parking. In many instances they are more like small budget hotels. Many guesthouses offer evening meals, but this may have to be requested in advance. Information is available from the Wales Tourist Board, where you can book online at www.visitwales.co.uk. Some of the best small hotels, inns and guesthouses can be found in the brochure published by **Great Little Places** ① *T01686-668030, www.wales.little-places.co.uk.*

Price codes

Where to stay

££££ over £160	**£££** £90-160
££ £50-90	**£** under £50

Prices include taxes and service charge, but not meals. They are based on a double room in high season.

Restaurants

£££ over £30	**££** £15-30	**£** under £15

Prices refer to the cost of a two-course meal, without a drink.

Bed and Breakfasts (B&Bs)

Bed & Breakfasts (B&Bs) provide the cheapest private accommodation. As their name suggests, they usually offer fairly straightforward accommodation in a private home, with a heart-stopping breakfast fry-up thrown in. Many are run by empty-nesters with beautiful period houses and gardens; elsewhere, the best of them tend to be on working farms. These days most have en suite or private bathrooms and TVs in the rooms – though do check beforehand to be sure. Again, their standards are extremely variable, but they're unlikely to cost much more than £80 per room per night, some as little as £50 – depending on their location as much as the quality they offer – and some hosts can really bring their area to life. Many hotels, guesthouses and B&Bs offer discounts for stays of more than one night, weekend deals, and high and low season prices. They can be booked through Tourist Information Centres (TICs). Some TICs charge a booking fee. Note that many B&Bs charge more than 50% of the room rate for single occupancy, so check beforehand.

Hostels

For those travelling on a tight budget, there is a large network of hostels offering cheap accommodation. These are also popular centres for backpackers and provide a great opportunity for meeting fellow travellers. Hostels have kitchen facilities for self-catering and some include a continental breakfast in the price or provide cheap breakfasts and evening meals. Advance booking is recommended at all times, and particularly from May to September and on public holidays.

In most major cities, national parks and other areas of outstanding natural beauty, budget accommodation can be found at **backpackers hostels** and **YMCAs**. Many campsites and youth hostels are run by the **Youth Hostel Association** ① *Trevelyan House, Dimple Rd, Matlock, DE4 3YH, T0800-019 1700, T01629-592700, www.yha.org.uk*. A bed in a dormitory usually costs about £15 a night.

Self-catering

One of the most cost-effective ways to enjoy Wales is to hire a cottage with a group of friends or family. There are lots of different types of accommodation to choose from, to suit all budgets, ranging from high quality serviced apartments and luxury homes to windmills and lighthouse keeper's houses and basic cottages with few facilities.

The minimum stay is usually one week in the summer peak season, though many offer shorter stays of two, three or four nights, especially outside the peak season. Expect to pay

Kiss and tell

If you hear anyone mention SWS, (pronounced soos), it stands for Social, Welsh and Sexy, www.swsuk.com – a sort of social club for ex-pat Welsh people and anyone else with an interest in Wales (you don't have to be sexy either). There are branches in London, New York and Moscow, and members include Catherine Zeta-Jones and Ioan Gruffudd. *Sws* is also Welsh for kiss. They've set up their own dating agency, www.cwtsh.com, but don't think you'll get a date with Ioan...

at least £200 per week for a two-bedroom cottage in the winter, rising to £400-600 in the high season, or more if it's a particularly nice place.

Some TICs and a large number of private organizations keep lists of self-catering options on their books. Two of the more interesting are the **Landmark Trust** ① *Shottisbrooke, Maidenhead, Berks, SL6 3SW, T01628-825925, www.landmarktrust.org.uk*, which rents out renovated historic landmark buildings, at a price; and the **National Trust** ① *36 Queen Anne's Gate, London, SW1H 9AS, T0844-800 2070, brochure line T0844-800 2072, www. nationaltrustcottages.co.uk*, which provides a wide range of accommodation on its estates, from an old rectory to a gas-lit cottage.

Contacts

Coast and Country Holidays, T01239-881297, www.welsh-cottages.co.uk.
Menai Holiday Cottages, T01248-717135, www.menaiholidays.co.uk.
Nefyn Holidays, T01758-720674, www.nefynholidays.co.uk.

Snowdonia Tourist Services, T01766-513829, www.sts-holidays.co.uk.
Wales Holidays, T01686-628200, www.wales-holidays.co.uk.

Campsites

There are plenty of campsites around Wales. Many are geared towards caravans and vary greatly in quality and level of facilities – some have large, luxury static caravans and electricity, others are just fields on a farm. The most expensive sites, which charge up to £25 to pitch a tent, are usually well equipped. Sites are usually only open from April to October.

Campus accommodation

Several Welsh universities open their halls of residence to visitors during the summer vacation (late June to September). Many rooms are basic and small with shared bathrooms, but there are also more comfortable rooms with private bathrooms, twin and family units and self-contained apartments and shared houses. Bed and Breakfast, and self-catering options are all available. Prices for B&Bs tend to be roughly the same as most B&Bs, but self-catering can cost as little as £50 per person per week. Local tourist offices have information, or contact the **British Universities Accommodation Consortium** ① *T0115-950 4571*, for a brochure. For Swansea contact T01792-295665, www.swan.ac.uk; and for Aberystwyth contact T01970-621960, www.aber.ac.uk.

Food and drink in Snowdonia and North Wales

Food

The quality of food in Wales has improved enormously in recent years. Since the 1980s the British in general have been shrugging off their reputation for over-boiled cabbage and watery beef and although the food revolution took a bit longer to reach Wales, the Welsh have now made determined efforts to improve the quality of food on offer. Annual awards are made to restaurants and pubs serving high-quality food, as well as to outstanding Welsh food producers. Although Wales has never had a cuisine that's particularly distinct to that of the rest of Britain, it does have some excellent local produce, such as lamb and fish, as well as a number of traditional native dishes. Organic produce is also widely available. Many chefs are now making the most of this, combining ingredients in imaginative ways, and creating lighter, fresher versions of traditional dishes to create what's generally known as 'modern Welsh' cuisine. An increasing number of contemporary restaurants, bistros and so-called 'gastropubs' (where the emphasis is on good food rather than boozing) are opening throughout the country. The cities also generally have Italian and Indian restaurants and most places, including pubs, will offer at least one choice for vegetarians. Not surprisingly, the capital Cardiff has the most cosmopolitan food culture and you can eat anything there, from Mexican to Japanese. You shouldn't go hungry in Wales as even the smallest places usually have a takeaway outlet, generally offering Chinese food, baked potatoes with fillings or, of course, fish and chips – which can be excellent if well cooked. The situation's not perfect and plenty of places still do fatty pies, greasy chips and overcooked veg but things are improving all the time.

So what should you look out for in Wales? Well, meat eaters can try Welsh **lamb** and Black **beef**, which have been farmed on the local pastures and hills for centuries. There is also salt marsh lamb, which is raised on coastal areas feeding on saline rich vegetation which gives it a distinctive, delicate flavour. Lamb is used to make *cawl*, a traditional broth made with leeks, potatoes and other veg.

Then there's a wide range of **seafood**, perhaps the best known of which are the Penclawdd cockles which are collected on the Gower Peninsula and sold at Swansea market. You'll also find oysters from Pembroke and Anglesey, crabs and lobsters from places like Milford Haven, and other delicacies like scallops and clams. The coastline, as well as Wales' lakes and rivers, mean that lots of fresh **fish** is available, from salmon to less familiar Arctic char and *sewin* (sea trout). The shore also gives Wales one of its most distinctive native dishes – **laver bread** (*bara lawr*). This is a sort of lettuce-like seaweed that is mixed with oatmeal and generally fried and eaten for breakfast with bacon – it's a Swansea favourite.

Lots of **vegetables** in Wales are produced organically – look out for the famous Welsh leek, often combined with potatoes in soups and stews. Then there are some wonderful Welsh **cheeses** varying from the famous Caerphilly, which is mild, white and crumbly to Llanboidy, a smooth, hard cheese. Most of the cheese-making production is in West Wales, especially the Teifi and Towy valleys. There are some delicious soft goat's cheeses available too. Hard cheeses are often flavoured with other ingredients such as laverbread, chives or garlic to create more intense flavours. Cheese, of course, features in some of Wales' native dishes such as **Welsh rarebit**, essentially cheese mixed with beer (or sometimes Worcester sauce) and grilled on toast, and **Glamorgan sausages**, made from cheese, herbs and vegetables.

Traditional Welsh baking recipes are simple but flavoursome. In tea rooms you might see **bara brith** (speckled bread), which is a sort of dried fruit loaf made with tea, and

Blue Flag beaches

The Blue Flag is an eco-label awarded to resort beaches and marinas throughout the world. Run by the independent non-profit organization **Foundation for Environmental Education** (FEE), the Blue Flag works towards sustainable development at beaches through strict criteria including water quality, environmental management, safety and facilities. Around 40 of Wales' beaches have been awarded Blue Flag status, for details see www.blueflag.org.uk.

Welsh cakes, which are made with fruit and cooked on a griddle. Welsh producers are also making **ice cream**, sometimes flavoured with local honey, yoghurts, preserves and handmade chocolates. Keep an eye out for them in delis and markets.

Eating out

For a cheap meal, your best bet is a pub, hotel bar or café, where you can have a one-course meal for around £7, though don't expect gourmet food. The best value is often at lunch time, when many restaurants offer three-course set lunches or business lunches for less than £15. You'll need a pretty huge appetite to feel like eating a three-course lunch after your gigantic cooked breakfast, however. Also good value are the pre-theatre dinners offered by many restaurants in the larger towns and cities (you don't need to have a theatre ticket to take advantage). These are usually available from around 1730-1800 till 1900-1930. The biggest problem with eating out in the UK is the limited serving hours in many pubs and hotels outside the main cities. These places often only serve food between 1230 and 1400 and 1700 and 1900, seemingly ignorant of the eating habits of foreign visitors, or those who would prefer a bit more flexibility during their holiday. In small places especially it can be difficult finding food outside these times. Check out www.uk-food-drink-travel.com for more information.

Drink

Drinking is taken as seriously in Wales as the rest of Britain and **beer** (flat, brown and made with hops) is still the national drink – although it faces serious competition from continental lagers and alcopops. **Real ale**, made from small independent breweries, is available in many pubs in Wales. Pubs are still the traditional places to enjoy a drink: the best are usually 'freehouses' (not tied to a brewery) and feature log fires in winter, pretty gardens for the summer, and thriving local custom. Those that also have accommodation are known as 'inns', while more and more are offering good food. The local brews are Brains beer, which is made in Cardiff and ale made at the Felinfoel brewery near Llanelli. As well as widely available 'bitter' you'll also find 'dark' in Wales, a sweeter, darker coloured beer.

Welsh **wines** are also now produced in the south, while the most recent additions to the local drinks industry are distilled drinks made in Penderyn near the Brecon Beacons. There's Penderyn Welsh **whisky**, Brecon gin, vodka and a creamy liqueur, www.welsh-whisky.co.uk. Pubs are usually open Monday to Saturday from around 1100-2230 or 2300, and on Sunday from around 1200-1500 and 1800-2230, though those in bigger cities might open for longer.

The eisteddfod

Meaning a 'meeting of bards' or 'a gathering' the eisteddfod (plural eisteddfodau) is a uniquely Welsh event. Its origins stretch far back in history to the days when poets, singers and musicians would gather to compete for positions in the households of the gentry. The first major eisteddfod was held in 1176 in Cardigan Castle and after that they were held regularly, until the practice began to die out in the 17th and 18th centuries. They were revived in the 19th century, the first modern one taking place at Carmarthen. Now they take place all over Wales, with two major annual festivals –

the International Musical Eisteddfod (www.international-eisteddfod.co.uk) and the Royal National Eisteddfod. The latter alternates between locations in north and south Wales and involves ceremonies in which prizes are awarded for poetry, prose, and music. Proceedings are conducted in Welsh and it's a fascinating insight into the country and its traditions. Visitors come from all over the world. The 2013 Royal National Eisteddfod will be held from 2-10 August in Denbighshire. The 2014 event will run from 1-9 August in Llanelli. Further details at www.eisteddfod.org.uk.

Festivals in Snowdonia and North Wales

Also check www.cerddystwyth.co.uk.
Jan Hen Galen (13 Jan). Celebration of 'Old New Year' according to the Julian calendar.
Mar St David's Day. Celebrations throughout Wales, on 1 Mar.
Jun Snowdon Fiddle Festival, Nantperis www.gwylffidil.info. Music festival held in little village of Nantperis.
Jul North Wales Bluegrass Festival, www.northwalesbluegrass.co.uk. Music festival held in Conwy.
Sesiwn Fawr, Dolgellau, www.sesiwnfawr.co. The 'mighty session' as it translates is a music festival held in Dolgellau.
Aug Machynlleth Festival, www.moma wales.org.uk. Well-established music festival held in The Tabernacle, Machynlleth.

Includes everything from classical to jazz, as well as Male Voice choirs.
Sep Abersoch Jazz Festival , www. abersoch.co.uk. Jazz festival on the Llŷn.

Public holidays

New Year's Day (1 Jan); **Good Friday** and **Easter Monday**; **May Day Bank Holiday** (the first Mon in May); **Spring Bank Holiday** (the last Mon in May); **Summer Bank Holiday** (the last Mon in Aug); **Christmas Day** (25 Dec) and **Boxing Day** (26 Dec). There are also local public holidays in spring and autumn. Dates vary from place to place. Banks are closed during these holidays, and sights and shops may be affected to varying degrees. Contact the relevant Area Tourist Board for more details.

Essentials A-Z

Accident and emergency

For police, fire brigade, ambulance and, in certain areas, mountain rescue or coastguard, T999 or T112.

Disabled travellers

Wheelchair users, and blind or partially sighted people are automatically given 34-50% discount on train fares, and those with other disabilities are eligible for the **Disabled Person's Railcard**, www.disabledpersonsrailcard.co.uk, which costs £20 per year and gives a third off most tickets. If you will need assistance at a railway station, call the train company that manages the station you're starting your journey from 24 hrs in advance. Disabled UK residents can apply to their local councils for a concessionary bus pass. **National Express** has a helpline for disabled passengers, T08717-818179, to plan journeys and arrange assistance. They also sell a discount coach card for £10 for people with disabilities.

Useful organizations include:
Disability Wales, T02920-887325, www.disabilitywales.org. The national association of disability groups in Wales.
Radar, T020-7250 3222, www.radar.org.uk. A good source of advice and information. It produces an annual National Key Scheme Guide and key for gaining access to over 9000 toilet facilities across the UK.
Tourism for all, T0845-124 9971, www.holidaycare.org.uk, www.tourismforall.org.uk. An excellent source of information about travel and for identifying accessible accommodation in the UK.

Electricity

The current in Britain is 240V AC. Plugs have 3 square pins and adaptors are widely available.

Health

For minor accidents go to the nearest casualty department or an Accident and Emergency (A&E) Unit at a hospital. For other enquiries phone NHS Direct 24 hrs (T0845-4647) or visit an NHS walk-in centre.

Language

Wales is officially bilingual and as soon as you enter the country you will be aware of this, with road signs and place names appearing in both Welsh and English. *Cymraeg*, as the language is known in Welsh, is spoken by around 500,000 people and is closely related to other Celtic languages like Breton and Cornish. The language has its heartlands in the north and west, particularly in places like Anglesey, the Llŷn Peninsula, Caernarfon and parts of Cardiganshire and Carmarthenshire; you're less likely to hear it in the capital Cardiff or in towns and villages along the border. For many people it is their mother tongue and you will have plenty of opportunities to hear this ancient language (probably the oldest in Europe) spoken. The language has received plenty of support, unlike Cornish which has been shamefully neglected. There is a Welsh language television station S4C (Sianel Pedwar Cymru): established in 1982 it broadcasts for several hours in Welsh each day. Shows include the long running BBC Welsh soap *Pobol y Cwm* or 'People of the Valley', set in the fictional village of Cwmderi. The digital S4C2 channel shows the proceedings of the Welsh Assembly, and viewers can choose to watch in English or Welsh. Welsh language radio includes the BBC's Radio Cymru and a number of commercial stations such as Radio Ceredigion, which is bilingual. More information on the BBC services at www.bbc.co.uk/cymru.

Money → *For up-to-date exhange rates, see www.xe.com.*

The British currency is the pound sterling (£), divided into 100 pence (p). Coins come in denominations of 1p, 2p, 5p, 10p, 20p, 50p, £1 and £2. Banknotes come in denominations of £5, £10, £20 and £50. The last of these notes are not widely used and may be difficult to change.

Banks and bureaux de change

Banks tend to offer similar exchange rates and are usually the best places to change money and cheques. Outside banking hours you'll have to use a bureau de change, which can be easily found at the airports and train stations and in larger cities. **Thomas Cook** and other major travel agents also operate bureaux de change with reasonable rates. Avoid changing money or cheques in hotels, as the rates are usually poor. Main post offices and branches of **Marks and Spencer** will change cash without charging commission.

Cost of travelling

Wales can be an expensive place to visit. Fuel is a major expense and won't just cost an arm and a leg but also the limbs of all remaining family members. Public transport – particularly rail travel if not booked in advance – can also be pricey, especially for families. Accommodation and restaurant prices also tend to be higher in more popular destinations and during the busy summer months. There is budget accommodation available, however, and backpackers will be able to keep their costs down.

The minimum daily budget required, if you're staying in hostels or camping, cycling or hitching (not recommended), and cooking your own meals, will be around £30 per person per day. If you start using public transport and eating out occasionally that will rise to around £35-40. Those staying in slightly more upmarket B&Bs or guesthouses, eating out every evening at pubs or modest restaurants and visiting tourist attractions can

expect to pay around £60 per day. If you also want to hire a car and eat well, then costs will rise considerably to at least £75-80 per person per day. Single travellers will have to pay more than half the cost of a double room, and should budget on spending around 60-70% of what a couple would spend.

Credit cards and ATMs

Most hotels, shops and restaurants accept the major credit cards though some places may charge for using them. Some smaller establishments such as B&Bs may only accept cash.

Currency cards

If you don't want to carry lots of cash, prepaid currency cards allow you to preload money from your bank account, fixed at the day's exchange rate. They look like a credit or debit card and are issued by specialist money changing companies, such as Travelex and Caxton FX. You can top up and check your balance by phone, online and sometimes by text.

Money transfers

If you need money urgently, the quickest way to have it sent to you is to have it wired to the nearest bank via **Western Union**, T0800-833 833, www.westernunion.co.uk, or **MoneyGram**, www.moneygram.com. The Post Office can also arrange a MoneyGram transfer. Charges are on a sliding scale; so it will cost proportionately less to wire out more money. Money can also be wired by **Thomas Cook**, www.thomasexchangeglobal. co.uk, or transferred via a bank draft, but this can take up to a week.

Opening hours

Businesses are usually open Mon-Sat 0900-1700. In towns and cities, as well as villages in holiday areas, many shops open on a Sun but they will open later and close earlier. For banks, see above. For TIC opening hours, see the tourist information sections in the relevant cities, towns and villages in the text.

Post

Most post offices are open Mon-Fri 0900 to 1730 and Sat 0900-1230 or 1300. Smaller sub-post offices are closed for an hour at lunch (1300-1400) and many of them operate out of a shop. Stamps can be bought at post offices, but also from many shops. A 1st-class letter weighing up to 100 g to anywhere in the UK costs 60p (a large letter over 240 mm by 165 mm is 90p) and should arrive the following day, while 2nd-class letters weighing up to 100 g cost 50p (69p) and take between 2-4 days. For more information about Royal Mail postal services, call T08457-740740, or visit www.royalmail.com.

Safety

Generally speaking, Wales is a safe place to visit. The larger cities have their fair share of crime, but much of it is drug-related and confined to the more deprived peripheral areas. Trust your instincts, and if in doubt, take a taxi.

Taxes

Most goods are subject to a Value Added Tax (VAT) of 20%, with the major exception of food and books. VAT is usually already included in the advertised price of goods. Visitors from non-EU countries can save money through shopping at places that offer Tax Free Shopping (also known as the Retail Export Scheme), which allows a refund of VAT on goods that will be taken out of the country. Note that not all shops participate in the scheme and that VAT cannot be reclaimed on hotel bills or other services.

Telephone → *Country code +44.*
Useful numbers: operator T100; international operator T155; directory enquiries T192; overseas directory enquiries T153.

Most public payphones are operated by British Telecom (BT) and can be found in towns and cities, though less so in rural areas. Numbers of public phone booths have declined in recent years due to the advent

of the mobile phone, so don't rely on being able to find a payphone wherever you go. Calls from BT payphones cost a minimum of 60p, for which you get 30 mins for a local or national call. Calls to non-geographic numbers (eg 0845), mobile phones and others may cost more. Payphones (few and far between these days) take either coins (10p, 20p, 50p and £1), 50c, 1 or 2 euro coins, credit cards or BT Chargecards, which are available at newsagents and post offices displaying the BT logo. These cards come in denominations of £2, £3, £5 and £10. Some payphones also have facilities for internet, text messaging and emailing.

For most countries (including Europe, USA and Canada) calls are cheapest Mon-Fri between 1800 and 0800 and all day Sat-Sun. For Australia and New Zealand it's cheapest to call from 1430-1930 and from 2400-0700 every day. However, the cheapest ways to call abroad from Wales is not via a standard UK landline provider. Calls are free using Skype on the internet, or you can route calls from your phone through the internet with JaJah (www.jajah.com) or from a mobile using Rebtel. Many phone companies offer discounted call rates by calling their access number prior to dialling the number you want, including www.dialabroad.co.uk and www.simply-call.com.

Area codes are not needed if calling from within the same area. Any number prefixed by 0800 or 0500 is free to the caller; 08457 numbers are charged at local rates and 08705 numbers at the national rate.

Time

Greenwich Mean Time (GMT) is used from late Oct to late Mar, after which time the clocks go forward 1 hr to British Summer Time (BST).

Tipping

Tipping in Wales is at the customer's discretion. In a restaurant it is customary to leave a tip of 10-15% if you are satisfied with the service. If the bill already includes a service charge, which is likely if you are in a large group, you needn't add a further tip. Tipping is not normal in pubs or bars. Taxi drivers may expect a tip for longer journeys, usually around 10%.

Tourist information
Tourist Information Centres (TICs)

Most cities and towns that you're likely to visit in Wales will have a local Tourist Information Centre (TIC), which can give you information on local attractions, restaurants and accommodation (including handling bookings – for a small fee) and help with visitors' enquiries, such as where to find an internet café. Many sell books, local guides, maps and souvenirs, and some have free street plans and leaflets describing local walks. In general, tourist offices tend to cater to those interested in taking tours or day trips, and are less useful if you're on a tight budget, in which case youth hostels can provide much the same information. See individual town information sections for lists of local TICs.

Museums, art galleries and stately homes

The **National Trust**, T0844-800 1895, www.nationaltrust.org.uk, plays an active role in protecting and managing stately homes, gardens and the countryside of Wales and owns 133 miles of the Welsh coastline. If you're going to be visiting several sights during your stay, then it's worth taking annual membership or investing in a **National Trust Touring Pass**, available for 7 (£23) or 14 (£28) days.

A similar organization is **CADW**, www. cadw.wales.gov.uk, the historic environment agency responsible for protecting and conserving Wales' historic buildings, parks, monuments, gardens, landscapes and underwater archaeology. *Cadw* (pronounced *cad-oo*) is a Welsh word meaning 'to keep'. If you're planning to visit a number of places, it may be worth buying a **CADW Explorer Pass**: 3-day pass £13.20, 2 adults £20.30,

family £28; 7-day pass £19.85, 2 adults £31.60, family £38.75.

Finding out more

A good way to find out more before your trip is to contact **Visit Britain**, which represents **Visit Wales** abroad. Their website, www.visitbritain.com, is very useful as a first-stop directory for accommodation. Alternatively, you can write to the head office at Brunel House, 2 Fitzalan Rd, Cardiff, CF24 4QZ. Both organizations provide a wealth of free literature and information such as maps, city guides, events calendars and accommodation brochures. Travellers with special needs should also contact their nearest Visit Britain office. For more detailed information on a particular area, contact the area tourist boards. **Tourist Information Centres** (TICs) exist in most Welsh towns and **National Park Information Centres** area good source of information for outdoor activities such as walking. Details are provided in the Ins and Outs section at the beginning of each area.

Useful websites

The official Welsh Tourist Board site and the various area tourist board sites have information on accommodation, transport and tourist sites as well as outdoor activities such as walking, skiing and fishing.

Travel and leisure

www.aboutbritain.com Useful links for accommodation and travel.
www.aboutwales.co.uk An encyclopaedia of information about Wales.
www.britannia.com A huge UK travel site. Click on 'Wales guide' for a massive selection of subjects plus links to various sites including newspapers.
www.bbc.co.uk The UK's most popular site with an excellent what's on guide.
www.data-wales.co.uk A wealth of facts and information on everything from festivals to pronunciation of Welsh names.

The Countryside Code

1 Drive carefully and behave courteously to other motorists and cyclists on narrow, winding roads. Park vehicles where they will not be a hazard or disruption to other motorists, residents or businesses.

2 Keep to public paths through farmland to minimize crop damage and avoid 'short-cuts' on steep terrain to prevent soil erosion and damage to vegetation.

3 Litter is an eye-sore, harmful to farm animals, wildlife and the water supply. Leave no waste and take all your rubbish home.

4 Protect wildlife, plants and trees.

5 Respect ancient monuments, buildings and sites of religious importance. Do not vandalize or cause graffiti.

6 Avoid damaging crops, walls, fences and farm equipment; leave all gates as you find them.

7 Do not collect wild flowers, seabird eggs or historical artefacts.

8 Avoid pollution of the water supplies – there are few toilets outside of villages so when walking in the countryside bury human waste and toilet paper in the ground and at least 30 m from water courses.

9 Guard against risk of fire from matches, cigarettes, stoves and campfires.

10 Keep dogs under control, especially when near to sheep at lambing-time, seabird nesting sites at cliff edges. Avoid dog-fouling in public places.

11 Respect the peace, solitude and tranquillity of the countryside for others to enjoy – keep noise to a minimum.

12 The landscape can be spectacular but dangerous – take particular care along precipitous cliff edges, hilltops and slippery coastal paths.

13 Stay away from working areas on the moors and hills during game shooting, lambing season, deer culling and heather burning, and respect other locally or nationally imposed access restrictions.

14 Report any damage or environmental concerns to the landowner or Natural Resources Wales, T0300-065 3000. or the Environment Agency's incident hotline T0800-807060 (Freephone, 24-hour service), www.environment-agency.gov.uk.

15 Be adequately prepared when you walk in the hills – check the weather forecast, carry warm, waterproof clothing and adequate food and water supplies, and know how to use a map and compass.

---

www.whatsonwhen.com Has a huge range of upcoming events around the world.
www.uktrail.com Provides comprehensive information on transport and hostels.
www.visitbritain.com Practical informative site with useful links and ideas.

Outdoors

www.ccw.gov.uk The Countryside Council for Wales provides information on nature reserves and walking and riding paths.
www.cycling.visitwales.co.uk Excellent site for touring or mountain biking; even shows how steep the climbs are.
www.goodbeachguide.co.uk How to check your kid won't be bathing in sewage. Lists facilities and activities for a large number of recommended UK beaches.
www.sustrans.org.uk Official site of the charity that coordinates the National Cycle Network. With a clickable, zoom-in map.
www.walkingworld.com Perhaps the best directory of British walks, although you have to pay to download their detailed maps.

History, politics and culture

See also CADW, page 24.
www.castlewales.com Information and links to over 400 castles throughout Wales.
www.onehistoricgarden.co.uk Information on 7 historic gardens in Wales which are currently being regenerated:

Walking in North Wales

Cambrian Way (www.cambrianway.com), 274 miles, the longest and toughest path from Cardiff to Conwy via Snowdon. Guidebook by Tony Drake, available from the Ramblers' Association.

Dyfi Valley Way, 108 miles, goes from Aberdovey to Bala lake (Lake Tegid) then round to Aberystwyth.

East Clwydian Way (www.ramblersnorthwales.org.uk), 122-mile circuit, start/finish Prestatyn. Guidebook by David Hollett, available from North Wales area of the Ramblers' Association.

Edge of Wales Walk (www.edgeofwales.co.uk), 95 miles from Clynnog Fawr along the pilgrim's route to the tip of the Llŷn Peninsula and Bardsey Island.

Glyndŵr'sWay (T01654-703376, www.glyndwrsway.org.uk), 132 miles, National Trail, opened in 2002, starts in Knighton, on the border and runs through Llandiloes, on to Machynlleth, then back through Llanwddyn and on to Welshpool. **The North Wales Path** connects Prestatyn and Bangor, with information from Conwy Countryside Service, T01492-575200.

Bryngarw Country Park, Margam Country Park, Penllergare Valley Woods, Cwmdonkin Park, Aberglasney Gardens, Scolton Manor and Colby Woodland Garden.

Volunteer work

www.btcv.org.uk The British Trust for Conservation Volunteers provides volunteer opportunities, themed events and activities throughout the year.

www.cat.org.uk The Centre for Alternative Technology near Machynlleth relies on volunteers to keep the centre running.

www.rspb.org.uk The Royal Society for the Protection of Birds is a UK charity working to secure a healthy environment for birds and wildlife; volunteer opportunities.

www.wwoof.org Willing Workers on Organic Farms, volunteer opportunities for those interested in the organic movement.

Visas and immigration

Visa regulations are subject to change, so it is essential to check with your local British embassy, high commission or consulate before leaving home. Citizens of all European countries – except Albania, Bosnia Herzegovina, Kosovo, Macedonia, Moldova, Turkey, Serbia and all former Soviet republics (other than the Baltic states) – require only a passport to enter Britain and can generally stay for up to 3 months. Citizens of Australia, Canada, New Zealand, South Africa or the USA can stay for up to 6 months, providing they have a return ticket and sufficient funds to cover their stay. Citizens of most other countries require a visa from the commission or consular office in the country of application.

The **UK Border Agency**, www.ukba.homeoffice.gov.uk, is responsible for UK immigration matters and its website is a good place to start for anyone hoping visit, work, study or emigrate to the UK. For visa extensions also contact the UK Border Agency via the website. Citizens of Australia, Canada, New Zealand, South Africa or the USA wishing to stay longer than 6 months will need an Entry Clearance Certificate from the British High Commission in their country. For more details, contact your nearest British embassy, consulate or high commission, or the Foreign and Commonwealth Office in London.

Weights and measures

Imperial and metric systems are both in use. Distances on roads are measured in miles and yards, drinks poured in pints and gills, but generally, the metric system is used elsewhere.

Contents

Footprint features

Snowdonia & North Wales

North Snowdonia National Park

Wales, for many people, is Snowdonia – particularly the land immediately surrounding Snowdon itself – the highest mountain in England and Wales. The national park was established in 1951 but Snowdon has attracted walkers, climbers, naturalists, poets and painters from the late 18th century onwards – when the beauty of 'sublime' mountain landscapes, once feared and avoided, first began to be appreciated.

Today Snowdonia, though stunning, can be a busy place and often lacks the 'away from it all' remoteness that you can still experience in the Highlands of Scotland. However, while Snowdon itself may attract many trippers, as well as casual walkers and serious climbers, other challenging peaks such as Tryfan, Glyder Fach and Glyder Fawr are less well trodden. And you don't just have to walk here; the varied landscapes of the national park make it an excellent place for loads of other outdoor activities, from scrambling to windsurfing.

Arriving in North Snowdonia National Park

Getting there and around

Snowdonia is easily reached by road, with links from the M6 to the M56 and A55 from the north, while the A487 and A470 get you there if coming from the south. The A5 runs through the heart of the area, from Shrewsbury across the border in England, direct to the bustling centre of Betws-y-Coed. Trains run from Llandudno Junction to Betws-y-Coed and Blaenau Ffestiniog. Some buses run from Betws to Capel Curig. You can take the **Ffestiniog Railway** to Porthmadog, where you can get services along the Cambrian coast. There is no doubt that, even though the roads can get very busy in high season, the car is the best way to get around, particularly if you're wanting to explore the area in depth. However the National Park Authority encourage more environmentally friendly ways of travelling and **Snowdon Sherpa** buses run around the main settlements such as Betws-y-Coed and Llanberis (see www.snowdoniagreenkey.co.uk). The **Explore Wales Pass** allows unlimited travel on mainline trains and buses. ▶▶ *See Transport, page 37. See also South Snowdonia National Park, page 54.*

Tourist information

Bala ⓘ *Pensarn Rd, T01678-521021, www.visitbala.org, Easter-Oct Fri-Tue (daily in Aug) 1000-1600.* **Betws-y-Coed** ⓘ *Royal Oak Stables, T01690-710426, www.betws-y-coed.co.uk, Easter-Oct 0930-1730, Oct-Easter 0930-1630.* **Beddgelert** ⓘ *Canolfan Hebog, T01766-890615, www.beddgelerttourism.com, daily Easter-Oct 0930-1730; Fri-Sun Nov-Mar 0930-1630.* **Llanberis** ⓘ *41b High St, T01286-870765, llanberis.tic@gwynedd.gov.uk, daily Easter-Oct 1000-1800, and weekends 1100-1600 in winter.* **Snowdonia National Park Authority HQ** ⓘ *Penrhyndeudraeth, Gwynedd, T01766-770274, www.eryri-npa.gov.uk; www.snowdonia-npa.gov.uk.* More information is available from www.visitsnowdonia.info.

Background

The Snowdonia National Park (Parc Cenedlaethol Eryri) is the largest in Wales and covers 840 square miles (2175 sq km), embracing areas as diverse as the craggy peaks of the mountains, and the sandy beaches of the Cambrian coast. However, when most people refer to Snowdonia they mean the mountainous area surrounding the park's focal point, **Snowdon** (Eryri). At 3560 ft (1085 m) it is the highest peak in England and Wales and a majestic draw for lovers of the outdoors. The first recorded ascent of Snowdon was in 1639, by Thomas Johnson in search of botanical specimens. The summit is known as *Yr Wyddfa* in Welsh, meaning 'the burial place', suggesting that the mountain held a fascination for earlier civilizations too. In later years the area has been used as a training ground for serious mountaineers, including those who conquered Everest. In 2009 a new visitor centre/café, **Hafod Eryri**, was opened on the summit. It replaced a 1930s structure and is built in contemporary style. See www.eryri-npa.gov.uk/visiting/hafod-eryri.

Betws-y-Coed and around → *For listings, see pages 36-37.*

Victorian travellers flocked to Betws-y-Coed (pronounced *betoos-ee-coyd*, often shortened to *betoos*). The village came to prominence following the establishment of an artists' colony in 1844. Waterfalls such as Swallow Falls and the Pont-y-Pair bridge were favourite subjects, while the coming of the railway in 1868 made this the premier tourist centre

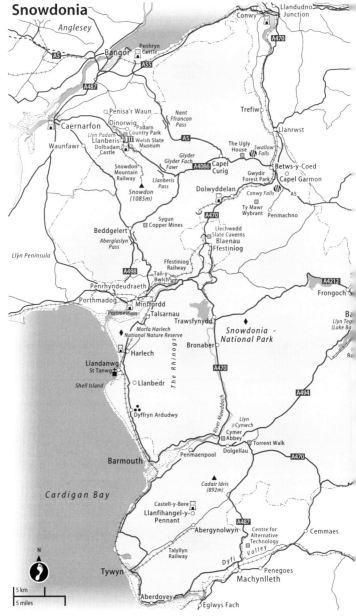

in Snowdonia. Tourists still fill the little streets today, though once they've had tea, browsed in the outdoor shops and bought some pottery, they've pretty much exhausted the village's possibilities. There's plenty of accommodation though and it's a convenient and pleasant base from which to explore Snowdonia. On the edge of the village you can see Thomas Telford's **Waterloo Bridge**, built in 1815. Made of cast iron it carries the emblems of the then newly United Kingdom: England's rose, Scotland's thistle, Ireland's clover and Wales' leek.

Other attractions in the village itself include the **Conwy Valley Railway Museum** ① *The Old Goods Yard, T01690-710568, www.conwyrailwaymuseum.co.uk, daily 1015-1700, £1.50, children 80p, family £4*, where kids can ride on a miniature steam railway. The village is really a base for walking and mountain biking. The best biking trails are in the **Gwydir Forest Park** (see What to do, page 37), while all types of walks are accessible, from tough climbs in the surrounding mountains to gentle woodland strolls.

A couple of miles west of the village, along the A5, is one of the area's most visited attractions: **Swallow Falls**. A draw since Victorian times, this pretty waterfall can only be reached through a turnstile (charge). Further along the road is **The Ugly House** or **Ty Hyll** ① *T01492-642322, www.theuglyhouse.co.uk, Apr-Oct daily 1030-1700 (tearoom and honeybee room Jan-Easter, Fri-Mon 1030-1600, Easter-autumn Tue-Sun 1030-1700), charge*, a cottage made from a haphazard arrangement of stones – it's said to date from 1475, when 'ty-un-nos' applied. This ancient law stated that a house would be yours if you built it overnight and had smoke coming from the chimney by morning; if you threw an axe from each of the four corners of the cottage the land delineated would be yours too. It used to be the headquarters of the **Snowdonia Society** ① *T01286-685498, www.snowdonia-society. org.uk*, but in 2012 opened as a visitor

Topping Snowdon

There are six major paths to the summit of Snowdon, the routes varying in difficulty. Before you tackle any of them or do any serious walking in Wales, make sure you are properly prepared with boots, warm and waterproof clothing (even in summer), maps (the best for walkers are OS Explorer 1:25,000), compass, food and water. Check weather conditions before setting off (www.metoffice.co.uk) and tell someone the route you intend to take. To give you an idea of how severe conditions can get think about this: Snowdon gets 200 ins (508 cm) of rain each year, the temperature can reach -20°C in winter, and the wind speed can reach 150 mph. A leaflet, *Stay Safe in Snowdonia*, is available from TICs. An app for safety advice is available to download from www.eyri-npa.gov.uk.

The most popular and easiest ascent is the **Llanberis Path**, which follows the Snowdon Mountain Railway and takes about three hours (descent about one to two hours). The other paths are the **Miners' Track**, the **Pyg Track**, the **Rhyd Ddu Path**, the **Snowdon Ranger Path** and the **Watkin Path**. There is also a serious ridgewalk, the **Snowdon Horseshoe**.

Of course you don't have to walk to reach the top of Snowdon (to the disgust of legions of outdoorsy types). Llanberis, starting point for many of the classic ascents of Snowdon, is also the starting point for the **Snowdon Mountain Railway** ① T0844-493 8120, www.snowdonrailway. co.uk, daily mid-Mar to Nov, weather permitting, £27 return, children £18, the narrow gauge railway (Britain's only rack and pinion railway) that runs nearly five miles up the mountain and has been operating since 1896. Once on the summit you can have a hot drink at Hafod Eyri, the new visitor centre, and in half an hour make the return journey. Book in advance in summer, if possible.

centre/tearoom. It is a centre for the protection of the Welsh honeybee and there is a display on the local breeding programme. The house also has a little garden, woodland walk and nature trail; it is close to the **Marin Trail**, a 25-km 'red' mountain biking trail. The Snowdonia Society runs a programme of walks and events; call or check their website for details.

From here the road leads to **Capel Curig**, the little village known to all walkers and climbers in Snowdonia. Standing at the gateway to the Llanberis and Nant Francon passes, it is a good base for exploring the surrounding mountains and there are several places to eat and stay, all heavily geared to hearty rucksack wearers. The village is the location of the **National Mountain Centre**, Plas y Brenin (see page 37).

South of Betws-y-Coed

To visit **Conwy Falls** ① T01690-710696, www.conwyfalls.com, charge, you enter through a turnstile by a pink-painted café, designed by Sir Clough William-Ellis and can then walk down through ancient woodland to see the stunning waterfalls and the remains of a Victorian fish ladder. Nearby are 30 km of mountain biking trails.

Northwest of Penmachno village, is **Tŷ Mawr Wybrant** ① (National Trust), A5 south of Betws, then B4406 to Penmachno, 2.5 miles from Penmachno, T01690-760213, Easter-Sep, Thu-Sun 1200-1700, Oct 1200-1600 (best call and check first), £3, children £1.50, family £7.50. This cottage is reached via a single track road that seems to last forever. It is an isolated spot, worth visiting for the delicious sense of remoteness alone. The cottage itself was the home of Bishop William Morgan (1545-1604), the man who first translated the whole of

A labour of love

Born in Ty Mawr, Penmachno in 1545, William Morgan studied at Cambridge, just a few years after an Act of Parliament was passed in 1563 by Elizabeth I to allow the translation of the Bible into Welsh 'because the English tongue is not understood [by]... her majesty's... obedient subjects inhabiting in Wales.' The first Welsh New Testament was produced in 1567 by Bishop William Salesbury, Richard Davies and Thomas Huet. However, they did not continue their task and the rest of the work passed to Morgan, by now Rector of Llanrhaedr-ym-Mochnant. He did so with enthusiasm, making himself so unpopular locally that he had to have an armed escort to and from the church, and preached his sermons with a pistol in his belt. In 1588, the first copies of the complete Welsh Bible were printed. This helped to ensure the future of the Welsh language and it is the basis of Welsh services today.

the bible into Welsh (see box, above). The house has been restored to its 16th-century appearance and has a display of Welsh bibles inside.

Dolwyddelan Castle ① *(CADW), Apr-Sep Mon-Sat 1000-1700, Sun 1130-1600, Oct-31 Mar Mon-Sat 1000-1600, Sun 1130-1600, £2.80, children £2.10, family £8.40*, was built around 1210-1240 by Llywelyn the Great to guard a mountain pass. The castle was restored in Victorian times and you get great views from the battlements. From Dolwyddelan village you can go for a walk along the river, or hike to the summit of **Moel Siabod** (2862 ft). In the village is **St Gwyddelan's Church**, built early in the 16th century with a seventh-century Celtic bell, Cloch Wyddelan.

Llanberis → *For listings, see pages 36-37.*

The busy lakeside village of Llanberis (www.llanberis.org) was once a centre of slate production and is the starting point for the **Snowdon Mountain Railway** as well as the most popular walking route up the peak, the **Llanberis Path** (see box, page 32). Now that the slate quarry has shut, the town is a mecca for walkers and climbers, cheerfully rustling in brightly coloured outdoor gear. Attractions include **Electric Mountain** ① *T01286-870636, www.electricmountain.co.uk, daily 1000-1630, Jun-Aug daily 0930-1730; last underground tour 1 hr before closing, tour price £7.75, children £3.95, family tickets available, no children under 4*, the lakeside visitor centre for the **Dinorwig Power Station**, a hydro-electric station housed in enormous caverns underground. An exhibition displays the 16th-century Peris Boat, and a 12th-century dugout canoe, unearthed during the building of the power station. Entry to the displays and cafés is free; the underground tour takes an hour – best to book in advance.

Padarn Country Park
① *T01286-870892.*

Padarn Country Park is an 800-acre park around the shores of Lake Padarn, once part of the Dinorwig Slate Quarry, which employed over 3000 local men until its closure in 1969. The workshops are preserved in the **Welsh Slate Museum** ① *T02920-573700, www. museumwales.ac.uk, daily, Easter-Oct 1000-1600, Nov-Easter, Sun-Fri 1000-1600, free*, as well as a reconstructed terrace of quarrymen's houses, moved from nearby Tanygrisiau, and a huge waterwheel. You can take a trip on the lake in a pleasure steamer, the **Snowdon Star** ① *T07974-716418, www.snowdonstar.co.uk, £6, children £4, family £18*, in summer. Trips start from a jetty near the Slate Museum. Also in the park is the **Llanberis Lake Railway** ① *T01286-870549, www.lake-railway.co.uk, daily Easter-Oct, £7.50, children £4.50, family tickets available*, a steam railway originally built to transport slate from the quarry. The five-mile journey runs between Gilfach Ddu station and Llanberis station.

Just south of the railway is the ruined **Dolbadarn Castle**, built in the 13th century by the mighty Llywelyn the Great. The castle predates the English fortresses of Edwardian conquest and provides solid evidence of the extent of Llywelyn's influence. Its simplicity and endurance has inspired artists such as Richard Wilson and JMW Turner.

Blaenau Ffestiniog → *For listings, see pages 36-37.*

When the Snowdonia National Park was established, the importance of industrial sites was not recognized. So although right at its heart, the slate mining town of Blaenau Ffestiniog isn't part of the national park itself. Yet it's one of the most interesting places to visit. Today, it's essentially a living museum for the world famous slate mining industry that brought the town prosperity in the 19th century. Although it has declined dramatically since the 1960s, slate still dominates the area, and if you arrive along the A470 from Betws-y-Coed the sudden appearance of this grey, forbidding landscape of shattered slate heaps can be depressing in the extreme. But it also has a harsh, dramatic beauty.

The **Ffestiniog Railway** ① *T01766-516024, www.festrail.co.uk, check for times, round trip £20.20, childen £18.20*, is a lovely narrow gauge railway built in the 1830s to transport slate from the quarries high up in Blaenau Ffestiniog down to the harbour at Porthmadog. Welsh slate was recognized as some of the finest in the world and in the 19th century was shipped everywhere, particularly for use as a durable roofing material. The trains originally ran downhill – fully loaded – pulled by gravity, and were pulled back up by horses when empty. In 1863 steam locomotives were introduced and passenger trains soon followed. By the 1920s new roofing materials had ousted slate and the industry declined dramatically; the line fell into disrepair and closed in 1946. Enthusiastic volunteers were determined to get it working again and in 1982 the line was re-opened. A ride on the train is a stunning experience, taking you round horseshoe bends, past lakes and waterfalls and through some of Snowdonia's most dramatic countryside. The train calls en route at **Minffordd**, **Penrhyn** and **Tan-y-Bwlch**. In Porthmadog it is now possible to take another vintage train on the **Welsh Highland Railway** ① *T01766-516024, www.festrail.co.uk, check for times, Porthmadog–Caernarfon single £22.70/return £34, children £20.40/£30.60*, which runs for 25 miles to Caernarfon (see page 45).

Blaenau Ffestiniog's other main attraction is the **Llechwedd Slate Caverns** ① *T01766-830306, www.llechwedd-slate-caverns.co.uk, Mar-Sep daily 0930-1730, last tour 1645, shorter hours in winter; free above ground; underground tours: tramway and deep mine £17, children £13; tramway or deep mine £10.50, children £8.50*. This slate mine gives you a real insight into the life of the miners and the importance of the industry to the town. The big pull are the underground tours for which you don hard hats: the Miners' Tramway takes you through slate caverns mined around 1846; the Deep Mine tour takes you underground on Britain's steepest passenger railway. Other attractions include a Victorian mining village with a cottage, inhabited until the 1960s; the working Miners' Arms pub; and a sweet shop, where you can change money into old currency and purchase sweets like gobstoppers.

Beddgelert → *For listings, see pages 36-37.*

Beddgelert, six miles west of Blaenau Ffestiniog, is easily the most attractive settlement in Snowdonia, with picturesque stone houses surrounded by majestic mountains and two gushing rivers running through the village. It is also the end of the beautiful **Aberglaslyn Pass**.

The most famous sight is the **Grave of Gelert** (*bedd* means grave in Welsh), the faithful dog who was said to belong to Prince Llywelyn. The story goes that the prince left the dog to guard his child, but when he returned he found the dog covered in blood, while the child was missing. Assuming the dog had killed the child, Llywelyn killed Gelert, then found the child lying safe with a dead wolf (that Gelert had bravely killed) nearby. You can see Gelert's grave under a lone tree, but it's believed the tale was made up in the 18th century by a local publican trying to attract tourists to the area – the place name instead referring to the grave of Celert, an early saint.

A short distance out of the village is the **Sygun Copper Mine** ① *T01766-890595, www.syguncoppermine.co.uk, daily Mar-Oct 0930-1700, £8.95, children £6.95*, where you can take an underground tour through tunnels veined with coloured ores and chambers of stalactites and stalagmites. There's also a small Celtic village, a room containing Bronze Age artefacts and a kids' playground.

Bala (Y Bala) → *For listings, see pages 36-37.*

Bala is 15 miles southeast of Blaenau Ffestiniog, reached via the A4212, on the edge of the national park. It sits by the largest freshwater lake in Wales **Llŷn Tegid** (Lake Bala), a noted spot for all sorts of watersports (see What to do, page 37). Just out of town is the **Bala Lake Railway** ① *T01678-540666, www.bala-lake-railway.co.uk, £9.50 return, family tickets available, 25 mins*, a narrow gauge, steam railway, which goes from Bala to Llanuwchllyn.

North Snowdonia National Park listings

For hotel and restaurant price codes and other relevant information, see pages 15-19.

🛏 Where to stay

Betws-y-Coed and around *p29*
££££-££ Bryn Tyrch Inn, Capel Curig, on A5, T01690-720223, www.bryntyrchinn. co.uk. 11comfortable en suite rooms. Ideally situated for walkers, climbers and cyclists, and with a pleasant, relaxed atmosphere. Evening meals and lunches available too.
££ Glyntwrog House, just south of Waterloo Bridge,15 mins' walk from the village, T01690-710930, www.glyntwrog snowdonia.co.uk. Established B&B, with clean and comfortable rooms. Walkers and cyclists welcome.
££ Henllys (The Courthouse), Old Church Rd, T01690-710534, www.guesthouse-snowdonia.co.uk. Former courthouse, now a B&B, that retains some of its original features – including an old holding cell.
££ Pengwern, Allt Dinas, T01690-710480, www.snowdoniaaccommodation.com. Lovely house 1 mile south of Betws-y-Coed, once used by visiting artists. Rooms are individually furnished and very comfortable. The Richard Gay Somerset room must boast the best loo-with-a-view in Britain. A former artist's studio is now a self-catering cottage.
££ Penmachno Hall, Penmachno, T01690-760410, www.penmachnohall.co.uk. 5-star country house in a former rectory. Lovely rural setting by the river.

Beddgelert *p35*
£££-££ Sygun Fawr, off A498, near Beddgelert, T01766-890258, www.sygun fawr.co.uk. 10 rooms, all en suite. Lovely old manor house in pretty gardens, close to Beddgelert village. Rooms are clean and comfortable, some with views over the mountains. Well worth seeking out. Excellent restaurant (see below).

🍴 Restaurants

Betws-y-Coed and around *p29*
£££-££ Bryn Tyrch Hotel, Capel Curig, on A5, T01690-720223, www.bryntyrchinn. co.uk. Bustling bar serving a wide range of meals, including an excellent choice of veggie/vegan dishes, such as spinach and chestnut tart.
£££-££ Stable Bistro, Royal Oak, Holyhead Rd, T01690-710219, www.stables-bistro. co.uk. The hub of the village. You can sit outside in summer and there's a wide range of food available. Live music is provided ranging from jazz to the local male voice choir.
££ Ty Gwyn, by Waterloo Bridge on A5, T01690-710383, www.tygwynhotel.co.uk. Attractive inn serving good bar meals. Very popular with locals and visitors. Best to book ahead.

Beddgelert *p35*
££ Sygun Fawr, off A498, near Beddgelert, T01766-890258, www.sygunfawr.co.uk. Popular guesthouse set in its own grounds and using lovely fresh produce. You'll need to book.
£ Glaslyn Ices, www.glaslynices.co.uk. Award-winning ice cream shop. Home-made sorbets and every flavour of ice cream from good old vanilla to chocolate and ginger or whisky cream.
£ Tanronnen Inn, T01766-890347, www. tanronnen.co.uk. Good choice of bar meals. Popular with locals and visitors.

⛰ What to do

Climbing
Beacon Climbing Centre, Waunfawr, 5-6 miles west of Llanberis, T0845-450 8227, www.beaconclimbing.com. Has an indoor climbing wall and offers short, taster sessions. 1½ hrs, £65 for 2 people. Also runs outdoor climbing courses in Snowdonia.

General outdoor adventure activities
National Mountain Centre, Plas Y Brenin, Capel Curig, T01690-720214, www.pyb. co.uk. Runs residential or 2-hr courses in everything from rock climbing and mountaineering to kayaking, canoeing and skiing. Geared to kids but adults welcome. Indoor climbing wall and ski slope.
Surf Lines Adventure Shop, Unit 2, Y Glyn, Llanberis, T01286-879001, www.surf-lines. co.uk. Offers activities from coasteering, climbing and guided trips to Snowdon. Also has canoes for hire.
Tree Top Adventure, Llanwrst Rd, Betws-Y-Coed, T01690-710914, www. ttadventure.co.uk. Offers a range of adventurous experiences from high ropes courses to climbing and canyoning.

Horse riding
Gwydyr Stables, Penmachno, near Betws-y-Coed, T01690-760248, www.horse-riding-wales.co.uk. Wide range of rides from 1 hr to full day, for all levels of ability.

Mountain biking
The **Gwydir Forest**, near Betws-y-Coed, offers some good biking including the 25-km Marin Trail. Further information on this and other trails is available from **Mountain Biking Wales**, www.mbwales.com. Mountain bike companies include:
Beddgelert Bikes, 1 mile outside Beddgelert, T01766-890434, www. beddgelertbikes.co.uk. Mountain bike hire, full day from £33, 2 hrs £15.
Beics Betws, Betws-y-Coed, T01690-710766, www.bikewales.co.uk. £28 per day.

Paragliding
Snowdon Gliders, Mynydd Llandygai, T01248-600330, www.snowdongliders.co.uk. Paragliding for all levels.

Watersports
Bala Adventure and Watersports, by TIC at Bala lake, T01678-521059, www.balawatersports.com. Windsurfing, kayaking, canoeing and land yachting.
Bala Sailing Club, The Foreshore, T01678-520118, www.balasc.org.uk. Offers sailing courses.
National Whitewater Centre, Frongoch, Bala, T01678-521083, www.ukrafting.co.uk. Whitewater rafting and kayaking. Also offers weekend adventure breaks with quad biking, tree-top adventure and canyoning. 2-hr to full-day experiences.
Padarn Boats, on Llŷn Padarn, Llanberis. Hires out rowing boats in summer, go to the green hut by the playground.

Transport

Betws-y-Coed and around *p29*
Snowdon Sherpa bus No S2 (www. gwynedd.gov.uk) runs to **Llanberis** and **Capel Curig**. Bus No 97 runs to **Capel Curig**, **Beddgelert** and **Porthmadog**.
 The Conwy Valley train line (www.conwy. gov.uk) runs between **Llandudno** and **Blaenau Ffestiniog.**

Blaenau Ffestiniog *p34*
Arriva Cymru buses 84 and X84 run between **Blaenau** and **Llandudno** (www.arrivabus.co.uk).
 The Ffestiniog Railway (see page 34) runs to **Porthmadog** and links the Conwy Valley and Cambrian Coaster lines. The Conwy Valley line runs several times daily to **Betws-y-Coed** and **Llandudno**. The Cambrian Coaster (www.the cambrianline.co.uk) runs between **Machynlleth** and **Pwllheli**.

Northwest corner and Llandudno

The northwest corner of Wales feels a world away from the chips and caravans of the north coast resorts like Rhyl and Prestatyn. It is the most traditional part of the country, where the Welsh language is spoken widely and where the Celtic past never seems far away. The genteel Victorian seaside town of Llandudno seems to mark the boundary between the raucous and the reflective. Once you reach the neat walled town of Conwy and see the brooding beauty of its castle, the change is palpable – both places provide a good base for exploring the area. Further west along the coast you come to the busy university town of Bangor and then to the heartland of Welsh nationalism, Caernarfon, famous for its castle. This corner of Wales also includes the two most characterful and isolated parts of the country: the beautiful Llŷn Peninsula and the pastoral island of Anglesey, last refuge of the Celts and rich in prehistoric sites.

Arriving in the Northwest corner and Llandudno

Getting there and around

Conwy and Llandudno are on the main A55 road. To the Conwy Valley, take the A470 or B5106. Buses that run along the north Wales coast stop at Conwy. There are regular trains from London and Birmingham to Llandudno Junction, where you can change for Conwy station. The **Conwy Valley Railway**, www.conwyvalleyrailway.co.uk, runs between Llandudno on the coast and Blaenau Ffestiniog in Snowdonia. The **North Wales Coast Line** from Chester runs to Bangor and Holyhead on Anglesey. **Cambrian Coaster** trains run to Porthmadog and Pwllheli on the Llŷn. The main towns of Conwy, Bangor and Caernarfon are small enough to be explored on foot. Buses run to the main places in Anglesey, however it is much easier with your own transport. For information on scenic train routes visit www.arrivatrainswales.co.uk.

Tourist information

Conwy ① *Muriau Buildings, Rosehill St, T01492-577566, conwytic@conwy.gov.uk, call for hours.* **Porthmadog TIC** ① *High St, T01766-512981, porthmadog.tic@gwynedd.gov.uk, Apr-Oct daily 1000-1800, Nov-Mar 1000-1700.* **Holyhead TIC** (Anglesey) ① *Stena Line Terminal, T01407-762622, www.anglesey.gov.uk, daily 0830-1800.* **Caernarfon TIC** ① *Oriel Pendeitsh, Castle St, T01286-672232, www.caernarfon.com, daily Apr-Oct 1000-1800, Nov-Mar daily except Wed 1000-1630.* **Pwllheli TIC** ① *Min y Don, Sgwar Yr Orsaf, T01758-613000, pwllheli.tic@gwnedd.gov.uk.* **Llandudno TIC** ① *Library Building, Mostyn St, T01492-577577, llandudnotic@conwy.gov.uk.* Useful websites: www.visitllandudno. org.uk, www.conwy.gov.uk.

Background

The Celts in the northwestern corner of Wales held out longer against the Roman invaders than anywhere else. The Druids, Celtic religious leaders, established a powerful base on the remote isle of Anglesey and it became an important spiritual centre. The Romans were held off until AD 61, when they massacred the Druids. The fall of the Roman Empire left a power vacuum and different parts of Wales were ruled by different leaders, all jostling for position. Those in the northwest, the Princes of Gwynedd, emerged as particularly powerful and extended their influence through much of Wales. But they were eventually defeated by Edward I, who left his stamp on the area when he built castles such as Conwy, Caernarfon and Beaumaris in his ruthless bid to bring the Welsh to heel. The area retains a stronger sense of a Welsh identity than other parts of the country and today Welsh is still the first language of the vast majority of people – particularly on Anglesey.

Llandudno → *For listings, see pages 51-53.*

Llandudno retains much of its Victorian character, when its dramatic setting, beaches, grand hotels, pier and shops attracted the great and the good. It's lively, but not tacky. The seafront sweeps in a lovely arc around Llandudno Bay and its sandy and pebbly beaches are overlooked by the mighty summit of the Great Orme (see below). Alice Liddell, who inspired Lewis Carroll's *Alice in Wonderland* books, used to holiday here with her family and a town trail of these connections is being developed. Carroll (alias the Reverend Charles Dodgson) often stayed with the Liddells and Alice used to join him on seaside walks.

Worth seeing is the **Oriel Mostyn** ⓘ *12 Vaughn St, T01492-879201, www.mostyn.org, Tue-Sun 1030-1700, free,* a contemporary art gallery, which has changing exhibitions of contemporary artworks, which could include film, installations and photographs. It also has a café. The **Llandudno Museum** ⓘ *17-19 Gloddaeth St, T01492-876517, Easter-Oct Tue-Sat 1030-1700 (closes for lunch), Sun 1415-1700; Nov-Easter Tue-Sat 1330-1630, £2,* has various exhibits associated with the town, from a footprint on a Roman tile to paintings and sculpture donated to the town. There's more on the past at the **World War II Home Front Experience** ⓘ *New St, T01492-871032, www.homefrontmuseum.co.uk, Mar-Nov Mon-Sat 1000-1630, Sun 10-1400, £3.25, children £2, family £9,* which focuses on civilian life in Britain during the Second World War. There's an old Anderson bomb shelter, a recreated wartime street, and plenty to learn about the work of the Home Guard, as well as rationing and the blackout.

The **Great Orme** itself, a huge limestone outcrop, can be reached on foot, by **tramway** ⓘ *Victoria Station, Church Walks, T01492-577877, www.greatormetramway.co.uk, daily late Mar-late Oct, £6 return, children £4.20,* or by taking the **cable car** ⓘ *Easter-Oct, daily 1000-1800; £6, children £4, family £16,* from Happy Valley. From here you get stunning views along the coast. It was settled as far back as Neolithic times and its rich mineral stores were mined as far back as the Bronze Age. **The Great Orme Bronze Age Copper Mines**

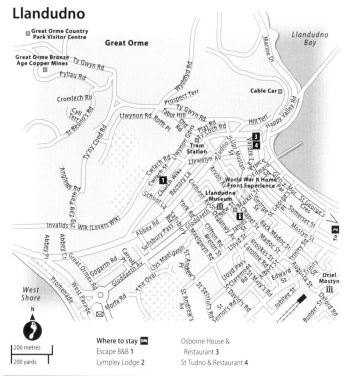

Llandudno

Where to stay 🛏
Escape B&B **1**
Lympley Lodge **2**

Osborne House &
Restaurant **3**
St Tudno & Restaurant **4**

ⓘ T01492-870447, www.greatormemines.info, Mar-Oct daily 1000-1700 (last tour 1600), £6.75, children £4.75, family £19, can be reached by tram from Victoria tram station or a short walk from the cable car. You get to don hard hats and go underground to explore these mines that were worked over 4000 years ago. There's a visitor centre depicting life in the Bronze Age.

The **Great Orme Country Park Visitor Centre** ⓘ T01492-874151, www.conwy.gov.uk/countryside, Easter-end Oct, daily 0930-1730, has displays and video on the area's history, geology and rich wildlife – over 400 types of plants grow here, some extremely rare. There's a live camera link up with a nearby seabird colony and information on the walks and nature trails on the Great Orme. At the **Summit Complex** ⓘ T01492-860963, there are places to eat and drink. There's also a **Ski and Snowboard Centre** (see page 53).

Conwy → For listings, see pages 51-53.

Conwy is a pretty little walled town dominated by a stunningly photogenic castle. With its well-preserved medieval charms, and picturesque setting on the Conwy Estuary, it's easy to see why it's a World Heritage Site. The town's history stretches back to Roman times at least, with settlers being attracted to the mussels that are still harvested there today. The castle is certainly the biggest draw but there are enough other attractions, shops and places to eat to occupy you for a day or two.

Constructed between 1283 and 1287, **Conwy Castle** ⓘ (CADW), T01492-592358, www.cadw.wales.gov.uk, Mar-end Jun, Sep-end Oct daily 0930-1700; Jul-Aug 0930-1800 daily; Nov-early spring Mon-Sat 1000-1600, Sun 1100-1600, £4.80, children £4.30, family £13.90, was

Conwy

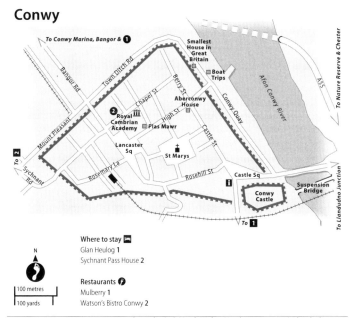

Where to stay 🛏
Glan Heulog **1**
Sychnant Pass House **2**

Restaurants 🍴
Mulberry **1**
Watson's Bistro Conwy **2**

one of the key fortresses in the 'iron ring' of castles built by Edward I to contain the Welsh. It took just four years to build at a cost of around £15,000 – about £9 million today – and its exterior, with eight huge round towers, is still largely intact. It's easy to see why it has long been a favourite subject for artists, including JMW Turner who painted it many times. Once inside, make sure you go up to the battlements, from which you'll get striking views of the surrounding mountains and of Conwy's well-preserved town walls, which stretch for around three quarters of a mile and are studded with 22 towers.

You can also see Conwy's old **Suspension Bridge** ① *T01492-573282, end Mar-Oct daily 1100-1700, charge*, built by Thomas Telford and opened in 1826. The bridge today is only used by pedestrians. The fee includes entry to the old Toll House, furnished as it would have been when inhabited around 1891.

From the bridge you can walk along **Conwy Quay**, where boat trips ① *T07917-343058, www.sightseeingcruises.co.uk, £6,* on the *Queen Victoria* leave for Llandudno. Wander upriver for views of the Conwy Valley, or visit the **Smallest House in Great Britain** ① *Apr-end Oct 1000-1800, charge.* This tiny dwelling has just two rooms yet was inhabited until 1900, the last resident being a 6-ft 3-in fisherman. You can squeeze inside and see the conditions for yourself.

The oldest house in Conwy is **Aberconwy House** ① *(National Trust), Castle St, T01492-592246, Mar-Oct, daily except Tue, 1100-1700, £3.40, children £1.70, family £8.50.* Built as a merchant's house it dates back to the 14th century and has rooms furnished in various periods of its long history. However, the most interesting property is fabulous **Plas Mawr** ① *High St, T01492-580167, Apr-Oct Tue-Sun 0930-1700, £5.75, children £4.35, family £17.25,* a superbly preserved Elizabethan house, built 1576-1585 for Robert Wynn, a prosperous Welsh merchant. Many of the rooms are decorated with elaborate plasterwork, designed to impress visitors in a 'come up and see my ceiling' sort of way. You can get an audio tour of the house, and there's also an exhibition containing horribly fascinating details of the contemporary diet – kids love it.

Art lovers should go to the nearby **Royal Cambrian Academy** ① *off High St, T01492-593413, www.rcaconwy.org, Tue-Sat 1100-1700, free.* It has changing exhibitions and displays contemporary paintings by artists such as Kyffin Williams, Maurice Cockrill and Ishbel McWhirter. As you go upstairs you're rewarded with a striking view of the castle.

Just outside town is an **RSPB Nature Reserve** ① *Llandudno Junction, T01492-584091, www.rspb.org.uk, daily 1000-1700, £3, children £1.50, family £6.50,* where there are extensive reedbeds, with hides and walks allowing you to spot reed buntings, reed warblers and sedge warblers, as well as many waders. There is also a visitor centre and café.

Vale of Conwy → *For listings, see pages 51-53.*

The lovely Vale of Conwy stretches from Conwy into the Snowdonia National Park to Betws-y-Coed. It's dotted with interesting villages and hamlets and has several good places to eat. **Bodnant Garden** ① *(National Trust), near Tal-y-Cafn, T01492-650460, mid-Mar to early Nov daily 1000-1700, £8.45, £4.22,* has lovely terraced gardens covering 80 acres of ground and dating back to the late 1800s – their most celebrated feature is the laburnum arch, on the left as you enter. Trefiw was once famed for **Trefiw Wells**, an ancient spa, with iron rich waters, believed to have been discovered by the Romans and later used by Victorian visitors. It's no longer open to the public.

Trefiw Woollen Mill ① *T01492-640462, www.t-w-m.co.uk, Apr-Oct daily, Nov-Mar Mon-Sat,* in Trefiw is a working woollen mill where visitors can see water turbines operating, and often see weaving and spinning taking place. The mill produces traditional bedspreads, tapestry throws and cushions.

Food lovers should head for **Bodnant Welsh Food** ⓘ *Furnace Farm, off the A470, T01492-651100, www.bodnant-welshfood.co.uk, Mon-Sat 1000-1800, Sun 1100-1700*. The farm shop stocks a wide range of Welsh food, much of it locally produced; there is also a tea room and a cookery school. The farm is also home of the National Beekeeping Centre for Wales and you can view demonstration hives and see beekeepers at work.

Llanrwst and around

South of Conwy along the A470, Llanrwst is a pleasant market town with several good places to eat and drink. The **Pont Fawr**, is an arched bridge attributed to Inigo Jones, the famous London architect who designed Covent Garden. It's often called the Buttermilk Bridge as the central arch, incorrectly fitted by drunken builders, collapsed soon after opening in 1636. The men were restricted to drinking buttermilk until it was safely rebuilt. The lovely ivy-clad building by the bridge is **Tu Hwnt I'r Bont** ⓘ *T01492-642322, www.tuhwntirbont. co.uk, open 1030-1700 mid-Mar to mid-Jun and Sep-Nov Tue-Sun; mid-Jun to Sep daily; Nov-Dec Sat-Sun*, which possibly dates back to the 15th century and was once the courthouse. Now it's a busy tea room. Take time to pop into **Gwydir Chapel** ⓘ *T01492-641687, daily 1000-1600*, beside St Grwst Church. Ascribed to Inigo Jones, it's the memorial chapel of the local Wynn family and contains a fascinating jumble of tombs, brasses and marble tablets. Look out for the stone effigy of a knight, and the underpart of the stone coffin of Llewelyn ap Iowerth (the Great), the son in law of King John whose coffin was brought here after the dissolution of Conwy Abbey. No one knows what happened to his body.

Just a short drive over the bridge is the Wynn family's former home, **Gwydir Castle** ⓘ *T01492-641687, www.gwydircastle.co.uk, guided tours available for groups if booked in advance*. A house existed here from the 14th century, though the building you see today dates from around 1500. It's still a family home and its current owners are gradually restoring this extraordinarily atmospheric building and its historic garden. The most striking room is the 1640's dining room, attributed to Inigo Jones, and covered with dark wood panelling and a rare gilded and silvered leather frieze. The interior was sold in 1921 to the American newspaper baron William Randolph Hearst, then passed to the New York Metropolitan Museum in 1956. They kept it locked away in packing cases and eventually, in 1996, it was purchased and returned to Gwydir. Bed and breakfast accommodation is available.

Bangor → *For listings, see pages 51-53.*

If you travel west along the coast from Conwy you reach the university town of Bangor, www.welcomebangor.co.uk, the largest town in Gwynedd and jumping off point for Anglesey. It was a popular destination in Victorian times and is a stop on the Chester–Holyhead railway. The town's **Victorian pier** stretches over 1500 ft into the Menai Strait and offers views of Thomas Telford's Menai Suspension Bridge which links the mainland to Anglesey.

The **Cathedral Church** ⓘ *Deiniol Rd, daily*, was founded by St Deiniol in AD 546, making it the longest continuously used cathedral in Britain. The original structure was destroyed by the Normans, and a later version sacked by the Vikings and rebuilt many times after that; the oldest surviving parts today date from the 12th century. The cathedral is noted for the carved oak figure known as the Mostyn Christ, thought to have been made in the 16th century. The cathedral was the site of the tomb of Owain Gwynedd and became a starting point for pilgrims setting out on the journey to Bardsey Island (see page 50). Outside the cathedral is a **Bible Garden** which contains plants with biblical connotations, such as the cypress variety said to have provided Noah with wood for his Ark.

The town's main museum is the **Gwynedd Museum and Art Gallery** ① *Ffordd Gwynedd, T01248-353368, Tue-Fri 1230-1630, Sat 1030-1630*, which contains a large collection of furniture, including some fine Welsh dressers, as well as other artefacts such as a Roman sword. The gallery has changing exhibitions of Welsh art but you can also see a painting of Caernarfon Castle by Sir Frank Brangwyn.

Around Bangor

Two miles east of Bangor is **Penrhyn Castle** ① *(National Trust), T01248-353084, Easter to end Jun, Sep-Oct Wed-Mon 1200-1700, Jul-Aug 1100-1700; grounds open from 1100 (Jul-Aug from 1000); garden only £6, children £3, castle and garden £10, children £5, family £25*. This extravagant castle is no ancient edifice, but was built in the 19th century in mock-Norman style for Lord Penrhyn, a wealthy Caribbean sugar plantation and slate quarry owner. There are over 300 rooms oozing stained glass, Norman-style furniture and a fine collection of paintings by artists such as Gainsborough and Rembrandt. There's even a massive slate bed that was built for Queen Victoria. The kitchens are laid out in Victorian style and there are extensive grounds which include an **Industrial Railway Museum**.

Nearby, the **Hendre Centre** ① *Lon Aber, Talybont, around 2 miles from Bangor off A55, T01248-371116, www.hendrehall.com*, is a 19th-century farmyard that was used as a staging post for cattle on their way to market. A venue for events and weddings, it also has workshops for local craftspeople and there are plans to open a café.

South east of Bangor, off the A5, is **ZipWorld Snowdonia** ① *Penrhyn Quarry, Bethesda, T01690-710914, www.zipworld.co.uk, tour takes around 2-3 hrs, £50, children £40, best to book in advance*. Situated in a vast slate quarry, the attraction has the longest zip wire in Europe. A guided adventure takes you on wires to the bottom of the quarry, which you then tour in a vehicle before ziplining back to the start.

Caernarfon → *For listings, see pages 51-53.*

Further south, along the coast from Bangor, is the town of Caernarfon, a stronghold of Plaid Cymru where a distinct dialect of Welsh is spoken – speaking English can sometimes make you feel unpopular. It is the site of the Roman fort of Segontium and is most famous for its magnificent **castle** ① *(CADW), T01286-677617, daily Easter to end May, Oct 0930-1700; Jun to end Sep 0930-1800; Nov-Easter Mon-Sat 0930-1600; Sun 1100-1600, £5.25, concessions £4.85, family £15.35*, an enormous structure, almost a town itself, built by Edward I from 1283. It stands at the mouth of the Seiont River overlooking the Menai Strait and was intended to be the focal point for Edward's dominance over the Welsh. It took around 40 years to build and is based around two oval courts divided by a wall, while the massive outer walls are 15 ft thick in some places. They're dotted with unique polygonal towers, and are made of limestone with strips of inlaid sandstone – features reminiscent of the city of Constantinople on which it was modelled. This was not just a fortress, it was the heart of Edward's imperial dream and it proclaimed him the conquering emperor, a theme continued in the magnificent eagles on the Eagle Tower – probably intended as the residential quarters of Sir Otto de Grandison, the king's representative. The castle also houses the **Museum of the Royal Welsh** (Wales' infantry regiment), formed from the merger of the Royal Welch Fusiliers (they used the ancient spelling) and the Royal Regiment of Wales. They fought at Waterloo and have a goat as their mascot, which is ceremoniously given a leek to eat each year. Beside the castle, in the old town, is **St Mary's Church**, which was founded in the early 14th century and is worth seeing for its Jesse Window.

Close to the castle is a new gallery/exhibition space, **Oriel Pendeitsh** ① *daily, summer 1000-1600, winter 1030-1530*, which focuses on the history of Caernarfon.

Just east of the centre, 10 minutes' walk along the A4085, is the **Segontium Roman Fort and Museum** ① *(CADW), T01286 675625, Apr-Easter Tue-Sun 1000-1600, museum daily 1230-1600, free.* Long before Edward I came to the throne, Wales was occupied by the Romans, who built this fort to subdue the locals and keep control of the area around Anglesey, the last outpost of the Druids. It was occupied from AD 78 until AD 394, longer than any other Roman settlement in Wales and was able to hold around 1000 infantry soldiers.

The **Welsh Highland Railway** ① *St Helen's Rd station, T01286-677018, www.festrail. co.uk, £34 return, concessions £30.60*, is another of Wales' lovely restored railways, this one runs from Caernarfon into the heart of Snowdonia – and then on to Porthmadog (see page 34). Restored steam engines haul you on this 25-mile journey, which goes by the foothills of Snowdon and the pretty village of Beddgelert.

Caernarfon

Anglesey (Ynys Môn) → *For listings, see pages 51-53.*

Across the Menai Straight is the island of Anglesey. The landscape is pastoral and so fertile that it was known as the 'breadbasket of Wales'. It's a great place to come if you're into prehistoric sites – the island is covered with them. The island's motto is 'Mam Cymru', meaning 'mother of Wales' and its great glory is the coastline, much of which is designated an Area of Outstanding Natural Beauty.

The island is linked to the mainland by Thomas Telford's **Menai Bridge**, which was built in 1826, the first permanent crossing of the strait. The bridge is 100 ft high so as to allow sailing ships with high masts to pass underneath. The second bridge across the strait was Robert Stephenson's Britannia Tubular Bridge, which carried trains over the water. It was damaged by fire in 1970 and little of the original structure remains as it was rebuilt in conventional style. The Victorian town of Menai Bridge is home to little **St Tysilio Church**, reached via a causeway. It was founded in AD 630.

In recent years the island's public profile has been increased due to the presence of the Duke and Duchess of Cambridge. The couple lived – and started their married life on – Anglesey because Prince William was working as an RAF search and rescue helicopter pilot, stationed at RAF Valley. They are due to leave the island in the summer of 2013.

Beaumaris (Biwmares)

Once the capital of Anglesey, the name is thought to mean 'beautiful marsh' in old French. It was once the chief port and commercial centre in North Wales, and in Victorian times became a popular resort. Moated **Beaumaris Castle** ① *T01248-810361, www.cadw.wales. gov.uk, Easter to end Jun, Sep, Oct daily 0930-1700; Jul, Aug 0930-1800; Nov-Easter Mon-Sat 1000-1600, Sun 1100-1600; £3.80, concessions £3.40, family £11*, was never completed – the money ran out – but it's a technical triumph, dating back to 1295. Built in concentric style, rather than with a traditional keep and bailey, the castle has inner walls up to 16 ft thick and 43 ft high. Its defences include 14 deadly obstacles, including cunning arrow-slits and 'murder holes' to defend entrances. It was once linked to the sea by its moat, which meant that it could be readily re-supplied by ships, which travelled along a channel in the surrounding marshes. In the Chapel Tower there's a small exhibition on Welsh castles.

The **Beaumaris Victorian Gaol** ① *Steeple Lane, T01248-810921, Easter to end Sep Mon-Thu and Sat-Sun 1030-1700, £4.60, children £3.60, family £15*, comprises Victorian punishment cells, dark secrets and dimly lit corridors. Prisoners were kept busy while confined in their cells, by cranking a handle up to 10,000 times a day – for no purpose other than to earn meals. People could be imprisoned for a month for stealing a quart of milk and public hangings were common. Close by is **Beaumaris Courthouse** ① *Castle St, T01248-811691, £4.60, children £3.60, family £15*, joint tickets with gaol available, which dates back to 1614 and has seen trials of everyone from murderers to petty thieves. It's the oldest active court in Britain and today most of the proceedings take place in Welsh.

Penmon

Around four miles north east of Beaumaris is **Penmon Priory** (unrestricted access), founded by St Seiriol in the sixth century. Viking raiders destroyed the original church and today you just see the remains of the 12th-century church and part of the cloister. The church contains two early carved crosses. Close by is **St Seiriol's Well**, said to have had healing properties. It has a huge dovecot, dating back to 1600 and able to house about 1000 birds. Under a mile from the Priory is little **Puffin Island**, once site of one of Anglesey's earliest monastic sites and now home to birds such as puffins and razorbills. You can take a one-hour cruise around the island from Beaumaris Pier; ask at the TIC for details.

Llanfairpwllgwyngyllgogerychwyrndrobwllllantysiliogogogoch

The most exciting thing about Llanfairpwllgwyngyllgogerychwyrndrobwllllantysilio-gogogoch, Llanfair PG or simply Llanfair (as it's known to locals) is its name – the longest in Europe. In English it translates as 'The Church of St Mary in the hollow of the white hazel near the rapid whirlpool and the church of St Tysilio near a red cave'. It was contrived as a marketing ploy by a 19th-century tradesman. All there is to see is the name at the railway station; it is still a stop on the Holyhead–Chester line.

Around Llanfair

Some 1.5 miles from Llanfair, on the A4080 is the magnificent building of **Plas Newydd** ① *(National Trust), T01248-714795, mid-Mar to end Oct Sat-Wed, house 1200-1700, gardens 1100-1730, £7.50, children £3.75, family £18.75; gardens only £5.50, children £2.75*. It was the home of the first Marquess of Anglesey who made a vast fortune from the copper mines at Parys Mountain on the island and was also the principal commander at Waterloo. The house dates back to the 16th century but was re-designed in the 18th century by James Watt, and is now a striking mix of classical and Gothic styles. The house is crammed with oil paintings, the most famous of which is Rex Whistler's enormous *trompe l'oeil* which takes up a whole wall and covers the mountains of Snowdonia, Portmeirion and even some London sights. There is also a **Cavalry Museum** which features the first Marquess's state-of-the-art wooden leg – he lost his leg at Waterloo. The house is surrounded by extravagant gardens and has a good tearoom.

Further along the A4080, about a mile northwest of Plas Newydd is **Bryn Celli Ddu** (unrestricted access), one of Anglesey's most important Neolithic sites. It was an important religious site and has been extensively researched by archaeologists. There's a surrounding stone circle and at the centre is a polygonal chamber where bones and arrowheads were found. Unfortunately the original stone was moved to the National Museum in Cardiff, so the one you see today is a replica.

If you've got kids in tow you might want to continue heading along the coast to **Anglesey Sea Zoo** ① *Brynsiencyn, T01248-430411, www.angleseyseazoo.co.uk, £7.50, children £6.50, family £26*. This is an absorbing aquarium with over 50 species and a chance to learn about different habitats. Displays include a Shipwreck and a Shark Pool, and there's an underwater camera giving you a fish's view of the world. There's also a chance to learn about seahorse conservation and a lobster breeding area.

Llanddwyn Island (Ynys Llanddwyn)

Llanddwyn Island, a peninsular in the southern corner of Anglesey, derives its name from St Dwynwen, the Welsh equivalent of St Valentine who lived during the fifth century and whose memory is commemorated on 25 January. The ruins of Dwynwen's Chapel can still be seen. **Dwynwen's Well** on the island is said to contain a sacred fish whose movements predict the fortunes of relationships. If the water bubbles it's said to be a sign of good luck. The island lies within the **Newborough Nature Reserve**. Canada geese, shelduck and red-breasted merganser are frequent visitors and over 550 different plant species including sea spurge (*euphorbia paralias*) and dune pansy (*viola curtisii*) have been recorded.

The beaches around **Malltreaeth** provided the inspiration for the wildlife artist Charles Tunnicliffe (1901-1979) who was famed for his studies of birds. Inland at Oriel Ynys Môn, is his recreated **studio** ⓘ *Rhosmeirch, Llangefri, T01248-724444, www.kyffinwilliams.info, daily 1030-1700,* the island's main gallery which covers the cultural history of the island. It also has a reconstruction of **Barclodiad y Gawres**, the most important Neolithic site in Wales. The original chamber is a 15-minute walk from Cable Bay, a couple of miles north of Aberffraw, off the A4080. Built around 3000 BC, the stones are decorated with spirals, chevrons and lozenges and the style is similar to stones in the Boyne Valley in Ireland. It is said that excavations have revealed remains of toads, snakes and shrews – as if used to concoct a mysterious magical potion. To visit the site get the key from the **Wayside Shop** in Trefaelog (deposit) and bring a torch.

Holyhead (Caergybi)

Holyhead, with its busy port, mainly serving Ireland, and bustling market (Monday 0800-1600) is the largest town on the island. In fact it's on a separate island – **Holy Island** – joined to Anglesey by a bridge. The island got its name as it was once settled by a monk St Cybi in the sixth century. His church is still here, on Stanley Street, built in the old Roman walls. The building today dates from the 13th century and contains stained glass by Arts and Crafts masters William Morris and Edward Burne-Jones. The **Holyhead Maritime Museum** ⓘ *T01407-769745, daily 1000-1600 in summer, closed winter, £2.50, children £1,* has displays on various aspects of seafaring and includes an exhibition of the sinking of the Royal Navy submarine *Thetis* in 1939, and of *HMS Scotia,* a ferry that was lost at Dunkirk.

West of the town is **Holyhead Mountain**, the highest point on Anglesey, which has an Iron Age hillfort on its summit. The Romans used this point as a watchtower and for communication with other beacons along the coast; a signal station was built here in the 19th century. A path leads from South Stack car park to the summit. On the clifftop is the **RSPB Ellin's Tower** ⓘ *T01407-764973, Easter-Sep daily, free,* from where you can watch some of the thousands of birds that nest on the cliffs: puffins, guillemots, razorbills and fulmars can all be spotted. Further west 400 steep steps lead down to a **lighthouse** ⓘ *T01248-724444, charge, Easter-Sep daily 1030-1730.* This was built in 1809 and visitors can now see the engine room and exhibitions, before climbing to the top for great views of the treacherous seas below.

A couple of miles south of Holyhead is **Trearddur Bay**, which has a Blue Flag beach (one of six on Anglesey) and is a good spot for surfing.

The Llŷn Peninsula → *For listings, see pages 51-53.*

The Llŷn Peninsula (pronounced *'thlinn'*) has a wonderful untamed appeal, particularly along the northern coast and remote tip, yet many visitors never get further than Porthmadog, the nearest town to the famous and gloriously eccentric village of Portmeirion. The area's main beauties are its unspoilt beaches, high banked lanes and sleepy churches – it's the sort of place that's great to explore on foot or by bike.

Porthmadog and around

Porthmadog takes its name from its founder, the MP William Madocks, who created a port linked by rail to the slate quarries at Ffestiniog, allowing vast quantities of slate to be shipped overseas. Rather unprepossessing, it's most notable as the southerly terminus of the delightful **Ffestiniog Railway** (see page 34). It's also a convenient base from which to explore the unique holiday village of **Portmeirion** ⓘ *T01766-770000, www.portmeirion-village.com, daily 0930-1930, £10, children £6, family from £30, discounts available online.*

Begun in 1926, this was the creation of the architect Clough Williams-Ellis, and fulfilled a childhood ambition to build an idealized village in a coastal setting. The village was designed around an Italian-style piazza, with a Liqorice Allsorts mix of buildings including Gothic, Classical and Italiante styles adorned with arches, fountains and statues. In 1941 Noel Coward wrote *Blithe Spirit* here as he came north to escape the bombs of the Blitz. The brightly coloured buildings make an arresting sight, but try and get here early in summer to avoid the coach parties. Many visitors are 'Prisoner' groupies, fans of the 1960's cult TV series *The Prisoner,* starring Patrick McGoohan, which was set here. As well as the village, there are 70 acres of woodland to explore.

Criccieth

This is a pretty Victorian holiday resort which snuggles beneath its ruined **castle** ⓘ *(CADW), T01766-522227, daily Easter-Oct 1000-1700; Nov-Easter Fri-Sat 0930-1600, Sun 1100-1600; £3.50, concessions £2.65, family £10.50, rest of year free access*. Originally built by Llywelyn the Great around 1230-1240, the castle was later taken over by Edward I, who extended and refortified it. It was eventually captured and burned by Owain Glyndŵr in 1404. There are panoramic views from the top and on a hot day it's worth bringing a book and settling down for a lazy hour or two. In the shadow of the castle is the **Chapel of Art** ⓘ *T01766-523570, Tue-Sat 1300-1700*, a restored chapel that shows contemporary Welsh art.

Llanystumdwy

A mile west of Criccieth is the childhood home of David Lloyd George, the charismatic Welsh social reformer who became British prime minister during the First World War. His home is now part of the **Lloyd George Museum** ⓘ *T01766-522071, www.gwynedd. gov.uk/museums, Easter 1030-1700, May Mon-Fri 1030-1700, Jun Mon-Sat 1030-1700, Jul-Sep daily 1030-1700, Oct Mon-Fri 1100-1600, £5, concessions £4, family £15*, which has a film about his life, as well as memorabilia ranging from Lloyd George teapots, to political cartoons – and even the thick yellow pencil with which he wrote his war memoirs. In the garden is the little cottage in which he was brought up, furnished much as it would have been during his lifetime.

Pwllheli

The main town on the Llŷn is Pwllheli (pronounced *'Poolth-heh-ly'*) which is most famous for being the place where the Welsh National Party, Plaid Cymru, was founded in 1925. It was once a thriving port but declined with the rise of Porthmadog. Three miles east of the town is **Penarth Fawr** ⓘ *Chwilog off A497, T01443-336000, daily 1000-1700, free*, which was built in the 15th century and is the only surviving hall house of that period left in the area. It was owned by members of the Welsh gentry and has a large hall with a fine timber roof. The stable block now houses various crafts and ceramics made by local Welsh craftspeople.

Llanbedrog

Llanbedrog, is a small but pleasant village with a lovely beach. It's notable for **Plas Glyn-Y-Weddw** ⓘ *T01758-740763, www.oriel.org.uk, daily 1100-1700, entrance fee*, a Victorian Gothic mansion that is now an impressive art gallery. With eye-stretching views out to sea, the house provides a grand setting for its changing exhibition of paintings (you may well find some Polish works on display as many Poles settled here after the Second World War and there are strong connections with Poland) and sculpture. In the Andrews Room is the permanent collection of porcelain, with Swansea and Nantgarw pieces.

Abersoch

The A499 road ends at Abersoch, a yachties haven, leaving the tip of the Llŷn to be explored by a lovely maze of 'B' and unclassified roads. Worth looking out for on the south coast is **Plas-yn-Rhiw** ① *(National Trust), Rhiw, T01758-780219, Easter to early May Thu-Sun 1200-1700; late May to end Aug Wed-Mon 1200-1700; Sep Thu-Mon 1200-1700, Oct Sat-Sun 1200-1600, £5.10, children £2.50, family £12.50*. This estate was once home to acclaimed Welsh poet R S Thomas who lived in a cottage on it. The main house is 16th century with some Georgian additions, and was derelict when it was purchased by friends of the poet, the Keating sisters. They restored it with help from Sir Clough William-Ellis and the house today contains many watercolours, painted by one of the sisters. The gardens are particularly fine, filled with wild flowers and run on organic principles. There are lovely views from the house across Cardigan Bay.

Aberdaron and Bardsey Island (Ynys Enlli)

Further along the coast is the little village of **Aberdaron**, where Thomas was minister. It used to be the last stop on the pilgrim trail to **Bardsey Island** (www.bardsey.org). This sits off the tip of the Llŷn, and has been an important place of pilgrimage since the sixth century when St Cadfan founded a monastery here. The Welsh name is Ynys Enlli, meaning 'Island of the Currents'– a reference to the treacherous tides that thrash around it. In the days when travel to Rome was difficult, it was said that three pilgrimages to Bardsey were equivalent to a trip to Rome. It was often known as the 'island of 20,000 saints', probably a reference to the large number of pilgrims who came here to die. The island contains the ruins of the abbey, but is most popular today with birdwatchers who come to watch the large numbers of nesting birds – Manx shearwaters and choughs are just some of the species that find sanctuary here. Trips to the island can be made from Aberdaron (T07971-769895, www.bardseyboattrips.com) or from Pwllheli (T0845-811 3655, www.enllicharter.co.uk). There are good views of the island from **Mynydd Mawr**, the hill at the very tip of the Llŷn.

The north Llŷn coast

The northern coast of the Llŷn is less populated than the south, and dotted with quiet beaches and sleepy churches. **Porth Dinllaen** is a little hamlet owned by the National Trust, which was once intended to be the main terminus for ferries to Ireland. One of the loveliest churches is the **Church of St Beuno** ① *Clynnog Fawr, May-Oct 1000-2000*, situated on an old pilgrims' route. Surprisingly large (Dr Johnson praised it as 'very spacious and magnificent for this country' in 1774) given its remote setting, it's a Tudor building but Christians have worshipped here since the seventh century. Inside are informative panels on the church and its history, as well as a parish chest of 1600, and some dog tongs, used to control badly behaved dogs in church. Nearby, at the crossroads at **Aberdesach**, a little road runs right down to a delightful hidden beach, a mix of golden sand, stones and seaweed. There's nothing but a few beach huts – it's a perfect place to paddle, stroll or just gaze out to sea.

Northwest corner and Llandudno listings

For hotel and restaurant price codes and other relevant information, see pages 15-19.

🍴 Where to stay

Llandudno and around *p39, map p40*

££££ Bodysgallen Hall and Spa, 3 miles inland from Llandudno off the A470, T01492-584466, www.bodysgallen.com. 15 rooms and several self-contained cottages set in extensive parkland. The house is 17th century and filled with antiques, and there are also spa facilities – the sort of place for a romantic weekend.

££££-£££ Osborne House, 17 North Parade, T01492-860330, www.osborne house.co.uk. Wonderfully indulgent, small seafront hotel that has suites with cast iron beds, Egyptian cotton sheets, Victorian fireplaces, luxurious bathrooms and widescreen TV with DVD.

££££-£££ St Tudno Hotel, North Parade, Promenade, T01492-874411, www.st-tudno.co.uk. Small, swish, luxurious hotel with a great location on the seafront. Alice Liddell (*Alice in Wonderland*) and her family once stayed here. Some rooms have sea views.

£££-££ Escape B&B, 48 Church Walks, T01492-877776, www.escapebandb.co.uk. Chic B&B, very cool and contemporary with individually designed rooms, flatscreen TVs and luxurious touches.

££ Lympley Lodge, Colwyn Rd, Craigside, T01492-549304, www.lympleylodge.co.uk. This 5-star B&B is set in its own grounds and has great views over the sea.

Conwy and around *p41, map p41*

£££ Sychnant Pass House, Sychnant Pass Rd, near Conwy, T01492-596868, www.sychnant-pass-house.co.uk. Wonderful and welcoming, award-winning country house with books, squashy sofas and individually decorated rooms, all of a very high standard. Meals on request.

££ Glan Heulog, Llanrwst Rd, T01492-593845, www.snowdoniabandb.co.uk. Good, clean and friendly B&B just outside the town walls.

££ The Grove, Fford Aber, Llanfairfechan, T01248-369111, www.thegrovenorthwales.co.uk. Friendly 5-star B&B in Edwardian detached house, convenient for exploring the coast of North Wales.

Vale of Conwy *p42*

££££-£££ The Groes Inn, 2 miles from Conwy on B5106, T01492-650545, www.groesinn.com. This old coaching inn claims to be the first licensed house in Wales, dating back to 1573. All rooms are individually furnished. The place has lots of character with log fires and wooden beams.

££ Gwydir Castle, on B5106 just outside Llanrwst, T01492-641687, www.gwydir-castle.co.uk. 2 rooms in an extremely atmospheric haunted medieval manor house, with oak panelling, antique furniture and baths so deep you could practically swim in them. 2-night minimum stay at weekends.

££ Yr Hafod, Trefiw, Llanrwst, T01492-640029, www.hafod-house.co.uk. A small hotel in the lovely Conwy Valley with comfortable rooms and a restaurant that is usually open a couple of nights a week.

Caernarfon and around *p44, map p45*

££££ Seiont Manor, Llanrug, 3 miles east of Caernarfon, T0845-072 7550, www.hand picked.co.uk/seiontmanor. The swishest hotel in the area with a large indoor pool, a gym and sauna. It's pricey but very comfortable.

££££-£££ Plas Dinas, Bontnewydd, T01286-830214, www.plasdinas.co.uk. Elegant hotel with pink washed walls and extensive grounds. Owned by the Armstrong-Jones family, it has individually styled rooms, Molton Brown toiletries and views across the Menai Strait.

££££-£££ Ty'n Rhos, Seion, Llanddeiniolen, near Caernarfon, T01248-670489, www.tynrhos.co.uk. Country house hotel overlooking the Menai Strait, with spacious rooms and good-quality food.

££ Plas Tirion Farm, Llanrug, 3 miles east of Caernarfon, T01286-673190, www.snowdoniafarmholidays.co.uk. Farmhouse B&B in a lovely rural location.

Anglesey *p46*
££££ Tre-Ysgawen Hall Hotel and Spa, Llangefni, T01248-758758, www.treysgawen-hall.co.uk. Grand old country house with Victorian features, and contemporary spa with pool, jacuzzi and pampering treatments.

££££-£££ Plas Rhianfa, Glyn Garth, Beaumaris, T01248-713656, www.plas rhianfa.com. Palatial country retreat in the style of a French chateau, with lavish rooms and a wood-panelled dining room.

£££-££ Ye Olde Bull's Head Inn, Castle St, Beaumaris, T01248-810329, www.bullshead inn.co.uk. Well-established inn that once welcomed Dr Johnson and Charles Dickens. Refurbished rooms in the adjoining Townhouse. Real fires in the bar.

££ Llwydiarth Fawr, Llanerchymedd, T01248-470321, www.llwydiarth-fawr.co.uk. Georgian farmhouse, with an open fireplace and lots of books. Good country breakfast.

££ Parc-yr-Odyn, Pentraeth, T01248-450566, www.parcyrodyn.com. Comfortable farmhouse B&B, with 2 self-catering cottages.

The Llŷn Peninsula *p48*
££££ Castell Deudraeth, Portmeirion, T01766-770000, www.portmeirion-village.com. Castle on the edge of town. Cool, sleek rooms and suites, less fussy and flowery than the main hotel and very comfortable.

££££ Plas Bodegroes, Pwllheli, T01758-612363, www.bodegroes.co.uk. Lovely Georgian manor house set in its own idyllic grounds. Also has a great reputation for food.

££££ Portmeirion Hotel, Portmeirion, T01766-770000, www.portmeirion-village.com. Plush rooms, suites and serviced cottages in the main hotel and dotted around the extraordinary village of Portmeirion.

££ Yr Hen Fecws, 16 Lombard St, Porthmadog, T01766-514625, www.henfecws.com. Once a bakehouse, this central restaurant with rooms has a comfortable, contemporary style.

🍴 Restaurants

Llandudno and around *p39, map p40*
£££ Paysanne, Station Rd, Deganwy, T01492-582079, www.paysannedeganwy.co.uk. A little bit of France in North Wales in this country-style French restaurant.

£££ St Tudno, North Parade, Llandudno T01492-874411, www.st-tudno.co.uk. Highly rated restaurant offering French-style food. Also noted for its afternoon teas.

£££-££ Bodysgallen Hall, off A470 near Llandudno, T01492-584466, www.bodysgallen.com. High-quality British food in a posh country house hotel. The Dining Room is for formal meals, while the Bistro offers more relaxed (and less expensive) dining. Afternoon teas are also available.

££ Nikki Ip's, 57 Station Rd, Deganwy, T01492-596611, www.nikkiips.com. Popular Chinese restaurant, with contemporary interior.

££ Osborne's Bistro, 17 North Parade, T01492-860330, www.osbornehouse.co.uk. Situated in Osborne's hotel, this bistro offers dishes such as fish pie, sautéed salmon and good vegetarian dishes.

Conwy and around *p41, map p41*
£££ Watson's Bistro Conwy, Chapel St, T01492-596326, www.watsonsbistroconwy.co.uk. Tucked away under the old town walls. Serves tasty lunches, which are good value, and contemporary evening meals such as ox cheek with savoy cabbage.

££ The Mulberry, Conwy Marina, T01492-583350, www.mulberryconwy.com. Pub serving varied bar meals such as fish and chips, and pasta dishes; good views over the new marina.

Vale of Conwy p42

£££-££ Groes Inn, Tyn-y-Groes, on B5106 about 2 miles from Conwy, T01492-650545, www.groesinn.com. Lovely 16th-century inn serving everything from sandwiches to venison pie.

££ Amser Da, 32-34 Heol yr Orsaf, Llanrwst, T01492-641188. Popular brasserie with a coffee bar out the front. Lots of local Welsh ingredients and everything from tasty sandwiches to heartier main dishes.

££ The Austrian Restaurant, Capuelo, 2 miles out of Conwy, T01492-622170, www.theaustrianrestaurant.com. Wed-Sat from 1800, Sun lunch from 1200. Authentic Austrian restaurant serving sustaining dishes like *wiener schnitzel* and *apfel strudel*.

££ Eagles Hotel, Llanrwst, T01492-640545, www.eagles-hotel.co.uk. This hotel is popular with locals and serves bar meals, Sun lunches and good thick chips.

Anglesey p46

£££ Cleifiog Ughaf, off Spencer Rd, Valley, T01407-741888, www.cleifioguchaf.co.uk. This country house hotel has a restaurant called **The Moody Goose**, which features lots of fresh local produce on the menu, such as line-caught cod. Pistachio and olive oil cake is a typical dessert.

£££-££ Lobster Pot, Church Bay, near Holyhead, T01407-730241. Tue-Sat 1200 1330, 1000 2100. Simple restaurant specializing in seafood sourced locally, such as lobster, crab, scallops and sole.

£££-££ Ye Olde Bulls Head Inn, Castle St, Beaumaris, T01248-810329, www.bullsheadinn.co.uk. Traditional pub serving modern British food.

££ Ship Inn, Red Wharf Bay, off A5025, T01248-852568, www.shipinnredwhardbay. com. This pub has lots of exposed beams and nautical knick-knacks. Welsh produce features in the menu.

The Llŷn Peninsula p48

£££ Castell Deudraeth, Portmeirion T01766-770000, www.portmeirion-village. com. Brasserie-style food in lovely setting. Welsh twist on meals such as Llŷn crab and Anglesey turbot.

£££ Plas Bodegroes, Nefyn Rd, Pwllheli, T01758-612363, www.bodegroes.co.uk. Crisp white tablecloths and high-quality food at this Georgian country house. Local produce cooked with imagination and flair.

££ Yr Hen Fecws, 16 Lombard St, Porthmadog, T01766-514625, www. henfecws.com. Come for breakfast of eggs Benedict, a light lunch or afternoon tea.

£ Caffi Cwrt, Y Maes, Criccieth. The best choice for traditional teas, scones and cakes in an atmospheric old building with wooden beams and a little tea garden.

⏼ What to do

Llandudno p39, map p40
Llandudno Ski and Snowboard Centre, Wyddfyd Rd, Great Orme, T01492-874707, www.jnlllandudno.co.uk. This centre has the longest toboggan run in Britain, as well as a PermaSnow ski slope. It also offers snowboarding and sno-tubing.

South Snowdonia National Park

Anyone who thinks the wildest parts of Wales are to be found in northern Snowdonia should think again. It is the southern part of the national park that boasts brooding Cadair Idris – the mountain that both horrified and inspired Romantic painters and poets – as well as the rough and empty Rhinogs, east of Harlech. Cadair Idris, or the Chair of Idris, was famously painted by Richard Wilson, and is a distinctive mountain on which survive rare alpine plants. The Rhinogs might not attract much attention, being below 2500 ft, but they still present some challenging walking – and are where Welsh walkers come when they want to escape the crowds that flock north to Snowdon. South Snowdonia is also etched with an almost unbroken stretch of superb sandy beaches, as well as historic towns such as Harlech, on the coast, and Machynlleth – once considered a likely capital of Wales – lying just outside the national park.

Arriving in South Snowdonia National Park

Getting there and around

The M4 from the south links with the A470 to Dolgellau and runs close to Machynlleth, while the northern stretch of the A470, linked to both the A55 and A5, joins the A496 which runs along the coast. Machynlleth and Harlech are both hubs for trains and buses, and there are good road links throughout. Both train and bus services run along the Cambrian Coast, and to Machynlleth, making travel between main centres relatively easy. The interior is most easily explored by car, although areas like the Rhinogs are not traversed by roads and must be explored on foot or bike. ▶▶ *See also North Snowdonia National Park, page 29.*

Tourist information

Harlech ⓘ *High St, T01766-780658, Easter-Oct daily 0930-1730, tic.harlech@eryri-npa.gov.uk.* **Dolgellau** ⓘ *Eldon Square, T01341-422888, tic.dolgellau@eyri-npa.gov.uk, Easter-Oct daily 0930-1730, Nov-Easter Thu-Mon 0930-1630.* **Barmouth** ⓘ *Station Rd, T01341-280787, barmouth.tic@gwynedd.gov.uk, Apr-Sep daily 1000-1800;* a useful website is www.barmouth-wales.co.uk. **Snowdonia National Park Authority HQ** ⓘ *Wharf Gardens, Aberdyfi, T01654-767321, tic.aberdyfi@eryri-npa.gov.uk, Easter-Oct daily 0930-1730, www.eryri-npa.gov.uk; www.snowdonia-npa.gov.uk.* Also see www.secretsnowdonia.co.uk.

Harlech and around → *For listings, see pages 59-61.*

Although it's small, Harlech punches above its weight, due to the presence of its gloriously dramatic castle and unspoiled golden sands. The town was once a fashionable resort attracting figures like Gustav Holst, Sir Henry Wood and George Bernard Shaw – nude bathing even started here in the 1930s. The swish **Royal St David's Golf Course** now attracts players from around the world.

Perched photogenically on a rocky outcrop, **Harlech Castle** ① *(CADW), T01766-780552, Apr-Jun, Sep-Oct daily 0930-1700, Jul-Aug daily 0930-1800, Nov-Mar Mon-Sat 1000-1600, Sun 1100-1600, £4.25, concessions £3.20, family £12.75*, was built by Edward I around 1283 after his conquest of Wales. It was once protected by the sea (which has now receded) but, despite its seemingly impregnable position, was captured more than once and had to withstand several long sieges. Owain Glyndŵr took it in 1404, it was recaptured, then was held by the Lancastrians for seven years during the Wars of the Roses – a feat that inspired the famous song *'Men of Harlech'*. The castle's battlements are extremely well preserved, and the short climb (on a clear day) is well worth it for the views across the sea and over to Snowdon.

Harlech's beach is excellent, with soft, clean golden sand – the sort of place where kids still make sandcastles and paddle without missing their computer games. The **Morfa Harlech National Nature Reserve** of sand dunes and estuary protects land where you can see wildlife such as redshank, shelduck and ringed plover.

A couple of miles away, set into the sand dunes at **Llandanwg**, is the fascinating little **Church of St Tanwg**. The church is Early Middle Ages, but gravestones have been found here dating back to the fifth century. The church was used until 1845 but then fell into disrepair. However, it was later restored and candelit services are sometimes held here. Further south is **Llanbedr** ① *www.llanbedr.com*, where there's a good pub and where a narrow road leads down to **Shell Island** ① *T01341-241453, www.shellisland.co.uk, daily Mar-Nov, £5 per car*, a peninsula cut off at high tide where you can go boating, birdwatching or fishing. There's also a restaurant and campsite.

There are a number of impressive prehistoric sites in this part of Wales, two of which can be seen south of Llandanwg at **Dyffryn Ardudwy** on the A496. A little path leads behind a school to the **Dyffryn Burial Chamber**, two Neolithic communal burial chambers sited close together.

Barmouth (Abermaw) → *For listings, see pages 59-61.*

Barmouth was once a busy port and there are reminders of its maritime heritage in the **Tŷ Gwyn Museum** ① *summer, daily, free*, with finds from local shipwrecks. It was here that Henry Tudor's uncle plotted his campaign against Richard III – resulting in Henry becoming Henry VII after the Battle of Bosworth. When the railway came to Barmouth in 1860, maritime trade declined and the town became a fashionable resort for genteel Victorians, attracted by the town's picturesque setting, squeezed beneath the cliffs at the mouth of the Mawddach Estuary. Today the town is more populist than picturesque, a bustling resort with a mishmash of amusements, busy bars and gift shops, in addition to the excellent Blue Flag beach and unspoiled surrounding countryside. It's popular with sailors, particularly each June when the **Three Peaks Yacht Race** (www.threepeaksyachtrace. co.uk) starts here. This gruelling race goes from Barmouth to Fort William, with contestants scaling the peaks of Snowdon, Scafell Pike and Ben Nevis along the way.

Walks on Cadair Idris

The steepest ascents are from the south, the easier ones from the north. Conditions on the mountain can change rapidly and you should always be well equipped and check weather reports locally before setting off. It's often said that anyone who spends the night on the summit will either wake up either mad or a poet. Dolgellau is a good base for walking on Cadair Idris.

The **Minffordd Path** (six miles) is the shortest but steepest ascent of the mountain. It starts from the car park at Minffordd, south of Dolgellau, goes up through the woods, then wheels round to the summit of Craig Cwm Amarch. The path then continues to the summit where there's a stone-built shelter, then heads east along a ridge to Mynydd Moel, where you make your descent.

The **Pony Path** (approximately six miles) is the classic ascent, starting from the car park at Ty Nant. You turn right onto the lane, then go left by the telephone box. The main path then leads to the summit. You descend past Gau Craig, down to Meas Coch Farm and back to the start.

The **Llanfihangel-y-Pennant Path** (10 miles) is the longest route. It starts at the hamlet of Llanfihangel-y-Pennant, takes you over the Afon Cadair then up the valley. Bear right at a col and follow the main path to the summit, then descend southeast.

Further information about these routes is available from: www.eyri-npa.gov.uk and www.walkingbritain.co.uk.

Above the town is **Dinas Oleu** ('fortress of light'), a gorse-covered hillside that in 1895 became the very first piece of land acquired by the National Trust. It was donated by Fanny Talbot, a philanthropist and friend of Octavia Hill, one of the founders of the trust. From this viewpoint you can pick up the waymarked **Panorama Walk**, which offers views of Cadair Idris, Barmouth Bridge and the coast.

The **Mawddach Trail** (www.mawddachtrail.co.uk) is a 9.5-mile (15-km) walking/cycling route that links Barmouth to Dolgellau. It follows a disused railway track that runs along the southern edge of the Mawddach Estuary.

From Barmouth you can get a ferry (charge) to **Penrhyn Point** where there's a sandy beach. Then you can connect to the narrow gauge **Fairbourne and Barmouth Railway** ⓘ *T01341-250362, www.fairbournerailway.com, day rover tickets £9, seniors £8, children £5.25 (£1 if accompanied), family £11.10*. This was laid out in 1895 by Arthur McDougall of McDougall's flour fame, transporting the materials used to construct the village of Fairbourne. Originally hauled by horses, the trains are now pulled by steam locomotives.

South of Barmouth

You'll find the resort towns of **Aberdovey** (Aberdyfi) and **Tywyn**, close to the green and scenic Dyfi Valley. Aberdovey is the prettier of the two, while Tywyn is home to the **Talyllyn Railway** ⓘ *T01654-710472, www.talyllyn.co.uk, daily end Mar-early Nov, some days in Feb, Mar and Dec, day rover £14.50, accompanied children £2.50, 8-day runabout fare £45.50, accompanied children £6*, a narrow gauge railway that steams seven miles through the countryside to the mountain halt of Nant Gwernol, **Abergynolwyn**. It was built to transport slate from the quarries to the coast. You can use the train to get to the starting point of a number of walks in the area, such as the **Pendre Station Walk** (four miles), and the **Dolgoch Falls**. At Wharf Station there's the **Narrow-Gauge Museum** ⓘ *T01654-710472, www.ngrm.org.uk, free,* which contains various locomotives and wagons from all over Wales.

In Tywyn you can see the **Church of St Cadfan**, said to have been founded in the sixth century. The eighth-century **Cadfan Stone** in the church has an inscription in Welsh and is said to be the earliest written example of the language.

A mile or so west of Abergynolwyn is **Llanfihangel-y-Pennant**. The hamlet contains the remains of the cottage of Mary Jones who, as a young girl, saved up for six years to buy a copy of a Bible from Thomas Charles, a Methodist preacher who had printed copies of William Morgan's Welsh Bible. She walked barefoot to Bala to get it. As he only had one copy left, he gave Mary his own and subsequently founded the Bible Society. You'll also find the ruins of **Castell-y-Bere** (around eight miles northeast of Tywyn). This is one of the few Welsh (as opposed to Norman) castles and was built in 1221 by Llywelyn the Great, with the aim of securing his southern border against rival princes. It was attacked by Edward I's forces in the 13th century and later abandoned.

Dolgellau → *For listings, see pages 59-61.*

At the head of the Mawddach Estuary, Dolgellau was accurately described in 1932 by HV Morton as "a hard little mountain town. Its houses are made of the mountains. They look as though they were made to endure forever." With its stone buildings and narrow streets, this pleasant market town seems to have changed little. It's full of history: Owain Glyndŵr assembled a parliament here in 1404, and in the 19th century it became a Welsh Klondike when the discovery of gold in the local rocks sparked a mini gold rush. The **Quaker Heritage Centre** ⓘ *Eldon Sq, T01341-424680, summer daily 1000-1800, winter Thu-Mon 1000-1700,* has an exhibition on the local Society of Friends, or Quakers. A community was established here in the 17th century and was, like other Quaker groups, persecuted for their non-conformist views. Many Welsh Quakers emigrated to Pennsylvania in the United States, establishing towns with Welsh names, such as Bangor.

Also on Eldon Square is **Ty Siamas** ⓘ *T01341-421800, www.tysiamas.com,* the National Centre for Welsh Folk Music. Situated in a grand Victorian building, the centre houses an exhibition, a recording studio, a shop and a café/bar. Live performances take place throughout the year.

Today Dolgellau attracts walkers and outdoor enthusiasts seeking a good base from which to explore nearby **Cadair Idris**, go cycling along the **Mawddach Trail**, fish in the rivers, or go birdwatching in the **Mawddach Valley** ⓘ *(RSPB), Dolgellau, T01654-700222.* There are plenty of walks to choose from including the **Torrent Walk** (two miles), along the banks of the Clywedog river, or the **Precipice Walk** (3.5 miles) round Llŷn Cynwch, which starts from the car park just off the road between Dolgellau and Llanfachreth and offers great views of Cadair Idris. North of Dolgellau is **Coed y Brenin**, which offers some of the best mountain-bike trails in Wales (see What to do, page 61).

Make time to seek out **Our Lady of Sorrows Church** on Meyrick Street, built by a determined Maltese priest, Francis Scalpell. He came to the town in 1939 when it was mainly Welsh speaking and began celebrating mass in an old stable. He eventually built a makeshift church with the help of Italian POWs but, determined to build something better, wrote 25,000 letters all over the world asking for funding. The money was eventually supplied by an anonymous stranger and the church opened in 1966.

West of town is Bontddu, where the famous **Clogau Gold Mine** ⓘ *www.clogaugoldmine. co.uk,* is situated (not open to the public). It opened in 1842 as a copper mine and gold was only discovered by accident in 1854. A nugget from this mine was used to provide the gold for the wedding rings of the Queen, the Queen Mother and Charles and Diana. The

Wales and film

The Hollywood actor Ioan Gruffudd hails from Cardiff, and Catherine Zeta Jones from nearby Mumbles; then there's the renowned Sir Anthony Hopkins, as well as Rhys Ifans and Matthew Rhys. With big names like that, it's not surprising that Wales has an increasingly fertile film scene. There's an excellent film school situated at Caerleon, near Newport, and Dragon Studios, a state-of-the-art film studio complex, are located near Bridgend. Some films are set in Wales, such as the cult film *Human Traffic* (1999), which was set in Cardiff. Welsh locations have long been used as a dramatic backdrop: the sand dunes of Merthyr Mawr in *Lawrence of Arabia* (1962); Raglan Castle in *Time Bandits* (1981); Caerphilly Castle in *Restoration* (1995), Snowdonia in the second *Tombraider* (2003). A number of big-budget Bollywood films have also been shot at locations in Cardiff, Caerphilly and the Brecon Beacons. The Brecons also featured in *King Arthur* (2004) which starred Keira Knightley, and Ioan Gruffudd as heroic Sir Lancelot, and in *Killer Elite* (2011) with Clive Owen and Robert De Niro. *The Libertine* (2005), a period romp starring Johnny Depp was shot at Tretower Court and Castle. Pembrokeshire's beautiful beaches are an enduring favourite with filmmakers: Marloes Sands was used in *Snow White and the Huntsman* (2012) with Charlize Theron, while Freshwater West was a location for Ridley Scott's *Robin Hood* (2010), and also featured in *Harry Potter and the Deathly Hallows* Parts 1 and 2 (2010/2011).

Duchess of Cambridge's wedding ring was also made of Welsh gold, although it is not clear whether it came from the Clogau mine.

A couple of miles north of town are the ruins of **Cymer Abbey**ⓘ *(CADW), daily 1000-1600, free*, a once isolated abbey (now sadly next to a caravan site). It was founded in 1198 by the Cistercians, an order that sought remote locations.

Machynlleth → *For listings, see pages 59-61.*

Pronounced *mah-khun-thleth* and just outside the Snowdonia National Park, this busy market town is a good base for exploring southern Snowdonia. With a reputation for being 'a bit hippy', 'Mac' as it's known to locals is a mix of galleries, pubs, wholefood shops and historic buildings. **The Owain Glyndŵr Centre** ⓘ *Maengwyn St, T01654-702827, www.canolfanglyndwr.org, Mar-end Sep 1000-1700, Oct-end Dec 1100-1600, £2.50*, is a 15th-century building where Owain Glyndŵr assembled a Welsh parliament in 1404. Now a heritage centre, displays cover Glyndŵr's life and explain his importance in Welsh history.

The Museum of Modern Art (MOMA) ⓘ *Penralt St, T01654-703355, www.momawales. co.uk, Mon-Sat 1000-1600, free*, is a cultural and performing arts centre with permanent displays of modern Welsh art and regular temporary exhibitions. There is a café and it is a venue for the annual **Machynlleth Festival** (see page 20).

Six miles south west of Machynlleth, off the A487 near Eglwys-fach, is **Ynys-hir Nature Reserve** ⓘ *visitor centre, T01654-700222, www.rspb.org.uk, Apr-Oct daily 1000-1700, Nov-Mar 1000-1600, closed Mon-Tue, £5, children £2.50*, a 1000-acre RSPB reserve set on the estuary with the Cambrian mountains behind. The habitats include salt marshes, woodlands, bogs and reed beds and there are seven hides and several nature trails. In winter you can spot wintering wildfowl like Greenland white-fronted geese, in spring and summer there are woodpeckers, lapwings and redshanks.

Centre for Alternative Technology
① *T01654-705950, www.cat.org.uk, daily 1000-1700 or dusk, entrance charge applies, reductions for those arriving by train.*

Three miles north of Machynlleth on the A487 (and the Sustrans 8 cycle route) the Centre for Alternative Technology deserves its reputation as one of the premier attractions in Wales – and despite its worthy sounding name, is certainly not just aimed at people who spin their own wool and know 101 ways with tofu. The centre was established in 1974 on an abandoned slate quarry, the idea being to build a self-sufficient community, both embracing and promoting 'green' technologies. You reach the centre via an extraordinary water-balanced cliff railway, similar to a cable car, and then watch an introductory video on the centre's establishment and ethos. The rest of the site is taken up with demonstrations of 'alternative' technologies and how they can be applied to modern urban living. There's a prototype low energy house, with displays asking you to think about everything from the distance your food has travelled, to using plants to improve air quality. Working organic plots demonstrate the principles of productive organic gardening, there are working solar panels and wind energy pumps, even a selection of eco toilets. There's also a good-value vegetarian café doing hearty soups, cakes and salads – allow a good half day for your visit.

South Snowdonia National Park listings

For hotel and restaurant price codes and other relevant information, see pages 15-19.

⊖ Where to stay

Harlech and around *p55*
££££-£££ Castle Cottage, High St, opposite TIC, T01766-780479, www. castlecottageharlech.co.uk. Family-run restaurant with rooms in the centre of Harlech. The modern Welsh cuisine of the restaurant is a feature.
£££ Tremeifion Vegetarian Hotel, Talsarnau, near Harlech, T01766-770491, www.tremeifionvegetarianhotel.com. Fabulous views from this exclusively vegetarian hotel. Dinner, bed and breakfast only, good food and a relaxed atmosphere.
££ Cemlyn, High St, T01766-780425, www.cemlynteashop.co.uk. Just 1 en suite room over this charming tea shop. Wonderful views of the castle.

Barmouth and around *p55*
£££-££ Ty'r Graig Castle, Llanaber Rd, T01341-280470, www.tyrgraig.castle.co.uk Striking Victorian house built as a summer retreat on a rock overlooking the town. Lovely stained-glass windows and wood panelling, and comfortable rooms.

South of Barmouth *p56*
££££-£££ Penhelig Arms, Terrace Rd, Aberdovey T01654-767215, www.penhelig arms.com. Popular local inn with a busy restaurant. Rooms are spacious and some have balconies with lovely views of the estuary. Dinner, B&B packages available.
£££-££ Llety Bodfor, Bodfor Terrace, Aberdovey, T01654-767475, www.llety bodfor.co.uk. Cool contemporary rooms at this boutique hotel. Rooms are airy with roll top baths, widescreen TVs and great views across Cardigan Bay. Good local food for breakfast and individual touches throughout.

Dolgellau and around *p57*

££££ Penmaenuchaf Hall, Penmaenpool, T01341-422129, www.penhall.co.uk. Grand manor house built for a wealthy cotton trader, now a country house hotel, with plush public rooms, a library and formal grounds.

£££-££ Plas Dolmelynllyn Hall, Ganllwyd, near Dolgellau, T01341-440273, www.dolly-hotel.co.uk. Victorian house on a lovely National Trust estate. Caters for walkers and mountain bikers and serves good local produce for breakfast.

£££-££ Y Meirionnydd, Smithfield Sq, Dolgellau, T01341-422554, www. themeirionnydd.com. This Georgian townhouse has light, pleasantly uncluttered guest rooms, free Wi-Fi and thoughtful touches of luxury. There's a good restaurant too, which is open to non residents.

Machynlleth and around *p58*

££££ Ynyshir Hall, Eglwysfach, near Machynlleth, T01654-781209, www.ynyshir. hall.co.uk. For real indulgence you can splash out at this luxurious hotel set in its own tranquil grounds, close to the Ynys-hir Nature Reserve. 9 suites are available, all individually decorated with thick carpets, swagged curtains and plump cushions.

£££ Minffordd Hotel, Talyllyn, near Tywyn, T01654-761665, www.minffordd.com. A 17th-century coaching inn that makes a great base for walkers as it's close to Cadair Idris. Log fires and old wooden beams, as well as good food.

££ Penrhos Arms Hotel, Cemmaes, near Machynlleth, T01650-511243, www.penrhosarms.com. Cosy rooms in this popular pub a few miles from the centre of town. Decor is light and bright, with antiques dotted around; 1 room has a 4-poster bed. The pub is a popular eating place too.

Restaurants

Harlech and around *p55*

£££ Castle Cottage, High St, T01766-780479, www.castlecottageharlech.co.uk. Restaurant with rooms serving evening meals, specializing in Welsh produce. Dishes might include local lamb, suckling pig or steak.

££ Cemlyn, High St, T01766-780425. This tasteful teashop serves a wide variety of teas. Team a pot with a rich brownie or freshly baked tiffin and relax on the little terrace.

Barmouth *p55*

££ The Bistro, Church St, T01341-281204, www.bistrobarmouth.co.uk. A wide range of dishes, including veggie options at this central bistro.

South of Barmouth *p56*

£££ Penhelig Arms, Terrace Rd, Aberdovey, T01654-767215, www.penheligarms.com. Seafront inn offering fresh fish dishes as well as vegetarian and meaty options, such as slow roasted pork belly with rhubarb and sage sauce.

Dolgellau and around *p57*

£££ Penmaenuchaf Hall, Penmaenpool, 1.5 miles west of Dolgellau, T01341-422129, www.penhall.co.uk. Elegant dining with fresh flowers and plush upholstery. Lots of game and local fish on the menu which features modern British dishes and fresh veg.

£££-£ Dylanwad Da, 2 Ffôs-y-Felin, T01341-422870, www.dylanwad.co.uk. Chalkboard menu that changes daily and includes the best local produce such as Welsh beef and lamb. It's a café/bar during the day and a restaurant at night.

££ Fronoleu, Tabor, on A470 near Dolgellau, T01341-422361, www.fronoleu. co.uk. Country restaurant with a relaxed atmosphere. Lots of local game and Welsh beef, as well as several veggie choices.

Machynlleth and around *p58*

£££ Ynyshir Hall, Eglwysfach, near Machynlleth, T01654-781209, www.ynshir hall.co.uk. Booking essential. If you can't afford to stay at this swish hotel you can maybe stretch to one of their highly rated meals. Herbs and veg fron their kitchen garden. Tell them in advance if you're veggie.

£££-££ Penrhos Arms Hotel, Cenmaes, near Machynlleth, T01650-511243, www.penrhosarms.com. The interior of this great pub is modern and simple, with plain wooden tables, stone walls and a fire in winter. There's a beer garden in summer. Bar meals might include Welsh black beef and mushroom pie, while mains in the restaurant might include grilled trout.

£££-££ Glan Yr Afon, Pennal, near Machynlleth, T01654-791285, www.river sidehotel-pennal.co.uk. This 16th-century inn has been transformed into a restaurant with rooms. It offers lunches and dinners, with a menu that changes with the seasons. Beef and ale pie is a typical dish.

££ The Black Lion, Derwenlas, A487, T01654-703913, www.theblacklion-machynlleth.co.uk. This 16th-century inn has lots of original features, log fires in winter and great pub food. Sunday roasts are popular and vegetarian specials available every day. Best to book.

⛰ What to do

General outdoor activities

CMC Pensarn Harbour, Llanbedr, T01341-241646, www.cmcpensarn.org.uk. Outdoor pursuits centre that does residential activities.

Mountain biking

Coed y Brenin, 5 miles north of Dolgellau off the A470, is a forest area with a range of excellent mountain biking trails. There's a fun trail for novices, a skills centre and several trails for more experienced and adventurous riders.
The **Visitor Centre**, T01341-440747, summer daily 0930-1700, rest of year Mon-Fri 0930-1640, weekends 0930-1700, has a café and information on the various routes, www.mbwales.com.

Quad biking

Madian Quads, Ty Mawr, Penegoes, Machynlleth, T01654-702746, www. westwales.co.uk. Offer 1- and 2-hr treks, some suitable for children over the age of 8.

Walking

The area offers everything from challenging walks on **Cadair Idris** (see box, page 56) and the **Rhinogs**, to gentle strolls through **Bron Y Graig park**, near Harlech.
Huw Gilbert Mountaineering, 2 Glasfryn, Corris, Machynlleth, T01654-761774, www.climbmountains.co.uk. Expert tuition for adventurous walkers wishing to learn more about scrambling, climbing and mountaineering.

Ceredigion Coast

The area known today as Ceredigion stretches south of the Dyfi Estuary to Cardigan and is a ribbon of coastal communities stretched out along Cardigan (Ceredigion) Bay. This western coast is the haunt of seals, sailors and students, dotted with hidden bays and pretty fishing villages. It's a great place to come for marine wildlife watching and there are some lovely beaches too. The main settlement is the Victorian resort of Aberystwyth, now a lively student town.

Arriving on the Ceredigion Coast

Getting there and around

The A487 trunk road runs between the main towns on this stretch of coastline linking Cardigan to Aberystwyth, and to Fishguard and Haverfordwest. Express buses run from Bristol and Cardiff to Aberystwyth. Trains from the Midlands run to Machynlleth, where you can then travel on to Aberystwyth. The narrow gauge steam **Vale of Rheidol Railway** can take you inland from Aberystwyth to Devil's Bridge, otherwise it is difficult to explore the more remote areas without your own transport. To travel between Aberystwyth and Cardigan you'll have to use buses, which link towns along the coast such as Cardigan, New Quay, Aberaeron and Aberystwyth. There are also links to locations inland such as Tregaron and Llandysul.

Tourist information

Aberystwyth TIC ① *Terrace Rd, T01970-612125, aberystwythtic@ceredigion.gov.uk, summer and bank holiday weekends daily 1000-1700, rest of year Mon-Sat 1000-1700, may close for lunch*. A useful website is www.discoverceredigion.co.uk.

Background

For most of its history Ceredigion was largely isolated from the rest of Wales by the Cambrian mountains, and the Welsh language, culture and sense of identity are still strong – though somewhat diluted by English settlers and visitors. The area was once an independent principality and takes its name from Prince Ceredig. Much of this beautiful area is designated Heritage Coast and is one of the best places to come to observe marine wildlife. It shelters some of Britain's rarest birds and is home to a resident population of bottlenose dolphins, as well as harbour porpoises and grey seals. The rivers and estuaries also provide superb wildlife habitats where you have the chance to spot wildfowl, rare plants and otters. Go further inland and you can see red kites which are fed daily.

Aberystwyth and around → *For listings, see page 68.*

Aberystwyth is both a student town and a resort. The university, founded in the 19th century, is now centred on a modern campus above the town, close to the National Library of Wales. The town grew from what is now the suburb of Llanbadarn Fawr, a settlement dating back to the sixth century when St Padarn established a monastic settlement here. It became a popular seaside resort from the early 19th century, the numbers of visitors increasing after the coming of the railway in 1864. Its promenade,

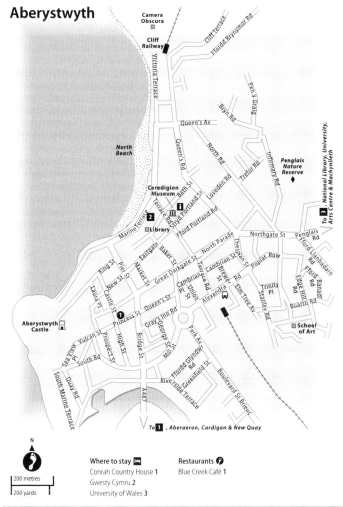

Aberystwyth

Camera Obscura
Cliff Terrace
Cliff Railway
Ffordd Brynymor Rd
Victoria Terrace
Pen y Graig
Bryn Rd
Queen's Av
North Beach
Queen's Rd
North Rd
Infirmary Rd
Tretor Rd
Penglais Nature Reserve
To 3 , National Library, University, Arts Centre & Machynlleth
Ceredigion Museum
Bath St
Terrace Rd / Ffordd Portland St
Loveden Rd
Ffordd Portland Rd
Marine Terrace
Library
North Parade
Northgate St
Penglais Rd
Ffordd Llanbadarn Rd
Eastgate
Baker St
Great Darkgate St
North Parade
Thespan St
Poplar Row
Ffordd Banadr
Edge Hill Rd
King St
Pier St
Market St
Terrace Rd
Cambrian Pl
Brewer Rd
Elm Tree Av
Trinity Pl
Stanley Rd
New St
Union St
Alexandra
Buarth Rd
Laura Pl
Castle St
Queen's St
Gray's Inn Rd
Park Av
School of Art
Aberystwyth Castle
Sea View Pl
Vulcan St
High St
Prospect St
Bridge St
George St
Mill St
Ffordd Glyndwr Rd
Riverside Terrace
Greenfield St
Boulevard St Brieuc
South Rd
Quay Rd
South Marine Terrace
A487
To 1 , Aberaeron, Cardigan & New Quay

N
200 metres
200 yards

Where to stay 🛏
Conrah Country House **1**
Gwesty Cymru **2**
University of Wales **3**

Restaurants 🍴
Blue Creek Café **1**

Owain's Uprising

One of the most important figures in Welsh history is **Owain Glyndŵr** (c1349-c1416), who led a mighty rebellion against English rule. He was an unlikely rebel, a wealthy man descended from the Princes of Powys and Deheubarth, who was well educated, studied law in London and even served in the English army: a pillar of the establishment. His rebellion stemmed from a prosaic dispute with his neighbour in the borders – Lord Grey of Ruthin appropriated a piece of his land and the courts refused to back Glyndŵr, treating him with great lack of respect. Infuriated, in 1400 he attacked the town of Ruthin with hundreds of Welsh supporters. It sparked a national uprising, with Welshmen living in England rushing home to support the cause. He attacked more towns in the north and later that year proclaimed himself Prince of Wales. Henry IV retaliated, not only with force but also by introducing a range of draconian laws forbidding the Welsh from holding public office, taking arms or holding assemblies. Not surprisingly, this fuelled support for the rebellion and Glyndŵr went on to take many castles, including Harlech. In 1404 he held the first Welsh parliament in Machynlleth, made alliances with France and Scotland, and was crowned King of Wales. However, the following year, when he made incursions over the border, he was beaten back by troops led by the king's teenage son – the future Henry V. In 1408, Harlech was taken by the king's forces and Glyndŵr was forced into hiding. He fled into the wilds of Snowdonia, and after that no one knows what happened to him – although he is known to have died by 1417. Only a mound remains of his birthplace Sycharth Castle, near Llangedwyn, north of Welshpool and no one knows where he is buried, but the Welsh will never forget his fight for freedom. See also History, page 73.

seafront Regency terraces and dowager hotels are constant reminders that this was once the 'Brighton of Wales'. Today it's a resort with a radical edge – a Nationalist town, home of the Welsh Language Society with a thriving art and music scene.

The former Coliseum theatre is now the opulent home of **Aberystwyth TIC** and **Ceredigion Museum** ① *Terrace Rd, T01970-633088, Apr-Sep Mon-Sat 1000-1700, Oct-Mar Mon-Sat 1200-1630, free*, which provides an unusual setting for a permanent collection on life in Victorian Wales, and changing exhibitions of art and crafts. From here you can walk along Marine Terrace to **Constitution Hill**, which rises 450 ft and is topped with a Camera Obscura – a cross between a telescope and a CCTV system with a 14-inch lens allowing you to look over the mountains and sea, and watch what's happening in town. It can be reached on foot or by the **Cliff Railway** ① *T01970-617642, www.aberystwythcliffrailway. co.uk, Mar-Nov, daily 1000-1700 (1800 Jul and Aug), £4 return*, which opened in 1896 and is the longest in Britain. Now powered by electricity, it was originally water balanced when it opened for Victorian pleasure trippers.

At the other end of town are the remains of **Aberystwyth Castle** ① *(CADW), free*, built by Edward I in the late 13th century. It saw plenty of action, withstanding several sieges including holding out for the king during the Civil War, until 1646 when its forces surrendered to Parliament.

Out of town is the **National Library of Wales** ① *Penglais Hill, T01970-632800, www. llgc.org.uk, Mon-Fri 0930-1800, Sat 0930-1700, free*, where extensive collections give a good insight into aspects of Welsh culture. The collection includes the oldest surviving manuscripts in the Welsh language, as well as the Welsh film and sound archive. Further up the hill is the **Arts Centre** ⓘ *T01970-623232, www.aberystwythartscentre.co.uk, galleries open Mon-Wed 1000-1700, Thu-Sat 1000-2000, Sun 1300-1700,* which houses the university's ceramic collection. There is also a shop and a café.

Penglais Road leads to the **Penglais Nature Reserve** set in a former quarry. It has a variety of tree and plant life, with a fine display of bluebells in the spring. Not far from the railway station in a fine Edwardian building, is the university's **School of Art** ⓘ *Buarth, Mon-Fri 1000-1300, 1400-1700, www.aber.ac.uk, free,* where you can see some examples of Welsh art from the university's permanent collection.

North of Aberystwyth

Five miles north of Aberystwyth, the resort of **Borth** comes alive in summer when its extensive sandy beaches become the haunt of windsurfers and kitesurfers. On the northern stretch of the sands, on the Dyfi Estuary, is the **Ynyslas Nature Reserve** ⓘ *visitor centre, T01970 871640, Easter-Sep, parking £1,* an extensive area of sand dunes that provides a home for wildlife such as lizards, voles, stoats, skylarks, ringed plovers and meadow pipits. There are many wildflowers and butterflies as well. The visitor centre has information on the wildlife and also on the two waymarked paths you can follow. At low tides you might see tree stumps sticking up through the sands, the remains of an ancient forest.

Vale of Rheidol

East of Aberystwyth, the Vale of Rheidol is a lush wooded valley most famous as the location of the **Devil's Bridge** and waterfalls – described by George Borrow in *Wild Wales* as "one of the most remarkable locations in the world" and a long-standing tourist trap. You can reach Devil's Bridge from Aberystwyth on the **Vale of Rheidol Railway** ⓘ *Park Avenue, T01970-625819, www.rheidolrailway.co.uk, Easter-Oct plus some special trips out of season, return £16, children £4,* a narrow gauge steam railway built in 1902 to serve the lead mines and passengers of the valley. The 11.75-mile journey through the gorgeous valley takes about an hour.

Cyclists might like to take the **Rheidol Cycle Trail** (17 miles, 27 km) which runs from Aberystwyth through the Vale of Rheidol to Devil's Bridge.

Devil's Bridge consists of three bridges stacked on top of one another, above the Mynach River. There's the 20th-century road bridge, below which is the Middle Bridge, erected in 1753, and the original Pont-y-gwr-drwg (Bridge of the Evil Man) which was built in the 11th century by monks from a nearby Cistercian abbey. Access to the bridges and the Devil's Punchbowl is by a turnstile (charge). On the opposite side of the road is the entrance to a nature trail and path which lets you see the bridges and the stunning **Mynach Falls** ⓘ *Easter-end Oct 0945-1700, charge, paid to attendant, otherwise insert money in coin-operated turnstile.*

Bwlch Nant Yr Arian Visitor Centre ⓘ *Ponterwyd, T01970-890453, daily 1000-1700 summer, 1000-dusk winter, parking charge,* gives access to waymarked walks and mountain bike trails, as well as a café. From the visitor centre you can see red kites swooping in to be fed (daily until 1500, 1400 in winter); in fact if you're on the A44 around that time you'll see the birds flying low over the roadway. You can do more birdwatching further north off the A487 at the RSPB's Ynys-hir Reserve (see page 58).

Just east of Bwlch Nant Yr Arian, the **Llywernog Silver-lead Mines** ⓘ *Ponterwyd, T01970-890620, www.silvermountainexperience.co.uk, mid-Mar to end Aug daily 1000-1730, last admission 1600, £12, children £9, family £38; prices for surface visit only £8, children £6,*

Kite country

Red kites are one of Britain's rarest birds of prey, but due to a stunningly successful protection programme they can be seen in many parts of Wales. The birds, with a wing span of up to 5 ft and a distinctive forked tail, were a familiar sight in the Middle Ages and a useful scavenger that kept the streets clean and kept down the numbers of crows; killing a kite attracted a capital punishment. They were known for their habit of stealing washing to line their nests – and are even mentioned by Shakespeare in *The Winter's Tale*. But from the 16th century onwards they began to suffer from persecution, particularly from gamekeepers. Birds were trapped, shot and poisoned, and egg collectors also targeted their nests – by 1900 their numbers had reached crisis point. They were extinct in England and Scotland, and only three or four pairs were left in Wales. In 1903 the first nest protection schemes were established by the Welsh and in 1905 the RSPB got involved. The tiny population just managed to hang on in Wales, but numbers continued to fall. By the 1930s only two breeding pairs were found – and the rarity of their eggs made them an even greater target for egg collectors. Their numbers increased

but only gradually: the introduction of myxomotosis in the 1950s poisoned the rabbits on which they fed, and the fact that Welsh kites are living in a marginal habitat means that they don't produce large numbers of chicks. In the 1960s more sophisticated methods of nest protection and monitoring allowed numbers to rise to around 20 pairs, and with support from farmers and other local people they continued to breed. Feeding programmes have played an important part in helping the birds to re-establish and the latest figures say there are 350-400 breeding pairs in Wales. The birds are still vulnerable and poisoning is a particular problem. In Wales this is often accidental but still devastating. Birds can die eating moles that have been killed with strychnine; from taking tainted carcasses left out to kill foxes and badgers; from ingesting lead shot left in dead birds and mammals; and from eating sheep that have died shortly after being dipped.

Red kites have now been re-introduced into England and Scotland, though still suffer from ignorant persecution there. The programme to protect them continues – it is the longest continuous conservation project in the world. See www.welshkite trust.org for further information.

family £26, drew speculators to the area in 1860. You can join an underground tour and try your hand at panning for minerals.

South of Aberystwyth

About 15 miles southeast of Aberystwyth is **Strata Florida Abbey** ① *Mar-end Oct daily 1000-1700, otherwise open 1000-1600 when entry is free, £3.50, concessions £2.65, family £10.50*, a Cistercian abbey founded in 1164 at a lovely spot in the Teifi Valley. Its name in Welsh 'Ystrad Fflur' means 'Valley of the Flowers' and refers to its original position a couple of miles away. The abbey became an important seat of learning and several Welsh princes are buried here, as well as Dafydd ap Gwilym a 14th-century poet – a yew tree is thought to mark his grave. The vast church (larger than St David's) was damaged by lightning in 1286 and was finally destroyed in the Dissolution. The setting is stunning, though little remains to be seen. The fine West Door survives, and remains of medieval

A rugby nation

Until their victory in the 2005 Six Nations Championship the Welsh rugby team had taken a bit of a battering. The glory days of the 1970s, when the Welsh game basked in the triumphs of players like Gareth Edwards and JPR Williams, had seemed well over.

The bell had appeared to toll for Welsh rugby with the arrival of professionalism in 1995. Once the game became a business, something of its gutsy spirit was lost, and Wales found it hard to find a foothold in this acquisitive commercial world. However, in recent years, Welsh rugby has regained its sparkle and there's a new confidence and pride in the game. The Millennium Stadium, a state-of-the-art venue, constructed bang in the centre of Cardiff, was built to replace the legendary Cardiff Arms Park, scene of many Welsh rugby wins (for 28 years the English side did not win once in Cardiff). In 2013 it was the venue for a decisive Welsh win over England, making Wales Six Nations' Champions – with full-back Leigh Halfpenny voted Player of the Championship.

Although hugely popular throughout the country, the notion of Wales as a rugby nation was never entirely accurate. In terms of clubs and top players, the game was mainly the preserve of the industrialized south. In the rural north, football (soccer), an import from nearby Liverpool and Manchester, took precedence.

So football versus rugby? Chances are the two passions will run side by side, just as they always have. Welsh Women's Rugby is also doing well. And if you want proof that the game still rouses intense passions, look no further than the Welsh rugby fan who, many years ago, was so convinced England would beat his team that he told his mates he would 'cut his balls off' if they won. Wales won – and he did. For further information look up **Welsh Rugby Union**, www.wru.co.uk.

tiled floors bearing symbols including a griffin and a fleur-de-lys. Legend has it that Joseph of Arimathaea took the Holy Grail from Jerusalem to Glastonbury, from where it then found its way to Strata Florida. After the Reformation it came into the hands of the Powells of the Nanteos Estate. An olive-wood artefact, known as The Nanteos Cup, became widely known and is thought to have inspired Wagner's opera *Parsifal*, after he saw it when he visited the house. Today the cup is thought to be hidden in a bank vault.

Ceredigion Coast listings

For hotel and restaurant price codes and other relevant information, see pages 15-19.

😴 Where to stay

Aberystwyth *p63, map p63*
££££ Conrah Country House Hotel,
Chancery, Rhydgaled, T01970-617941,
www.conrah.co.uk. Luxurious hotel, set
in its own grounds about 3 miles from
town. Fresh flowers from the garden,
antiques dotted around and all the
comforts you'd expect.
££££ Nanteos Mansion, Rhydyfelin,
2 miles outside Aberystwyth, T01970-
600522, www.nanteos.com. Stunning
Georgian mansion set in extensive grounds,
that has been restored and turned into
a luxury hotel with just 4 rooms, 10 suites
and a separate Mews cottage. The sort of
place to come for a special treat.
££££-££ Gwesty Cymru, 19 Marine
Terrace, T01970-612252, www.gwesty
cymru.com. This seafront townhouse
in Aberystwyth has 8 stylish modern
guestrooms, bathrooms with walk-in
showers, and free Wi-Fi.
££ Cwmwythig, Capel Bangor, 4 miles
east of Aberystwyth, T01970-880640,
www.cwmwythigholidayswales.co.uk.
This working dairy farm offers B&B as well as
self-catering accommodation for low prices.

🍴 Restaurants

Aberystwyth *p63, map p63*
£££ Conrah Country House Hotel,
Chancery, Rhydgaled, T01970-617941.
This is the place to come for a formal meal
in lovely surroundings. Food is modern
British using local produce, including
vegetables from the hotel garden.
£££ Gwesty Cymru, 19 Marine Terr,
T01970-612252, www.gwestycymru.com.
Seafront restaurant with rooms, with a
menu featuring lots of Welsh produce
cooked with a contemporary twist –
think lamb shank braised in Cambrian
ale, rosemary and orange.
£££ Nanteos Mansion, Rhydyfelin, 2 miles
outside Aberystwyth, T01970-600522,
www.nanteos.com. Classy food at this
luxury hotel which serves afternoon tea, as
well as lunch and dinner to non residents.
££-£ Y Ffarmers, Llanfihangel y Creuddyn,
T01974-261275, www.yffarmers.co.uk.
Some 8 miles south east of Aberystwyth.
This country pub offers an excellent choice
of bar lunches and evening meals. Local
produce features strongly and there are
plenty of vegetarian options – such as
cheese, beetroot and spinach pie.

Cafés
£ Blue Creek Café, Princess St, T01970-
615084. Cosy but uncluttered café. Lots
of good choices for veggies, other dishes
include 'posh beans on toast' served with
bacon, rocket and parmesan.

Contents

Background

History

Prehistory

There is evidence of human settlement in Wales as far back as 250,000 BC when a human tooth was discovered at Pontnewydd in North Wales. It is thought that these ancient Neanderthal inhabitants lived in small groups as hunter-gatherers and made little impact on the area. By **Palaeolithic** times, man appeared to be establishing more significant settlements and the remains of a skeleton, christened the **Red Lady** (actually a man), discovered at Paviland Cave on the Gower, have been dated variously at 24,000 or 16,500 BC. **Mesolithic** peoples left little for archaeologists to find, but the Neolithic settlers who followed them left traces which can still be seen today. The **Neolithic** colonists, short, dark people, sometimes called Iberians, came from the Mediterranean area. They were the first farmers and established settled communities, clearing forests, constructing villages – and building circles of standing stones (henges) and vast burial chambers for their dead. The best known of these is Stonehenge in Wiltshire, made from bluestones hacked from the Preseli Hills in Pembrokeshire, but Wales is littered with such mysterious monuments including Pentre Ifan in Pembrokeshire and Bryn Celli Ddu in Anglesey.

The Neolithic period morphed gradually into the **Bronze Age**, with its use of metals to make implements and pots, and increasingly sophisticated social structures. Hillforts (defended villages) began to appear, then around 600 BC the **Celts** arrived.

The Celts

The Celts originally came from the area around the Rhine in Europe. A tall, fair people with sophisticated social structures, they made a huge impact. They were noted for their love of war and imposed their ways on the existing tribes of Britain very quickly. They used iron, rather than other metals, were artistically skilled and had distinctive religious beliefs – with their religious leaders, the **Druids**, enjoying huge power. Caesar wrote of Celtic society that there were 'only two classes of men who are of any account…the common people are treated almost as slaves …the two privileged classes are the Druids and the Knights'. They also brought with them a new language which had two distinct strands: **Goidelic** (the basis of the Celtic languages in the Isle of Man, Scotland and Ireland) and **Brythonic** (the basis of Cornish and Welsh).

Celtic tribes established themselves throughout Wales: the Silures in the southeast, Ordovices in the northwest, Demetae in the southwest and Cornovii and Deceangli in the northeast. The Celts flourished until the arrival of the Romans, who first came to Britain in 55 BC, and finally conquered much of it in AD 43.

The Romans

The Celtic/British tribes continued to fight the Romans, notably Boudicca's Iceni in eastern England, who spread throughout the country. Tribal leader Caratacus (Caradog) moved west to organize resistance but it was hard, as the tribes here weren't as socially cohesive as in the south and east. The only uniformity was provided by the powerful Druids, whose stronghold was in Anglesey, described by Roman writer, Tacitus, as the place where young men from all over Europe were trained for the 'priesthood'. However, the rougher landscapes of the west helped keep the Romans at bay and it was not until after AD 75, when the massive fort was built at Caerleon (Isca), that they could be said to have conquered Wales.

The Romans built roads throughout Wales, linking important forts at Caernarfon (Segontium) and Carmarthen (Moriduum), and settled down for a long occupation. Gradually their sophisticated language and ways of living – and later their new Christian religion – started to influence local Celtic culture. Essentially a stable Romano/British culture emerged which ended with the decline of the Roman Empire.

The Dark Ages

As the Roman Empire floundered it became increasingly difficult to defend isolated areas such as the western parts of Wales. The long, exposed coastline meant that Wales was subject to raids from Ireland in the west, with further incursions from the Picts in the north and the Saxons in the south. By the end of the fourth century the Romans no longer ruled Wales. Britain became subject to increasing raids from warring **Teutonic** tribes who established themselves in the south and east of England. **Christianity**, which had only taken a tenuous hold through the Romans, returned to Wales during the fifth and sixth centuries, with the arrival of missionaries from Ireland. **Illtud** introduced the idea of Celtic monasticism and established a religious school at **Llantwit Major** in south Wales; in AD 500 his pupil **St David** founded St David's cathedral in Pembrokeshire.

Around the same time, Irish settlers (who spoke the Goidelic tongue) began moving into western parts of Wales, but were expelled from the north by **Cunedda**, leader of the Brythonic speaking Votadini (Gododdin) tribe. Well organized, they established themselves in north Wales and gradually spread as far south as the Teifi. They set up the royal house of **Gwynedd** and consolidated the Brythonic language in Wales. By the sixth century a distinctive **Welsh language** was evolving. Latin was used for formal affairs like legal matters, but everyday speech was Welsh. The earliest known example of written Welsh is on an eighth-century stone.

The Welsh coast was also subject to raids from **Vikings**, who left their stamp in place names such as Skomer. The tribes in the west, who saw themselves as **Cymry** (compatriots), became isolated. Wales – which had been given an obvious border in the late 700s when **King Offa** built the great earthwork Offa's Dyke, to delineate his Mercian territory – began to develop a distinct identity.

In AD 856 **Rhodri Mawr** (the Great) beat off the Vikings and created a largely unified Wales, although as the practice of primogeniture (first born male inherits) did not apply in Wales, inheritance squabbles meant it was never as stable as England. More Viking raids in the mid-ninth century served only to increase links with England for defensive reasons, but Rhodri's grandson **Hywel Dda** (the Good) became king of most of Wales. He was the first Welsh ruler known to issue his own coins and is also recognized as the codifier of **Welsh Law**. After his death, the country descended into anarchy, only coming together under the rule of **Gruffydd ap Llywelyn** – who even managed to grab some lands off Edward the Confessor – before being killed by his own people at the behest of Harold, Edward's successor.

The Norman Conquest

The first Norman castle in Wales was built in 1067 at **Chepstow** and the Normans gradually encroached on Welsh lands. By the end of the 11th century they had reached Pembroke in the south and other parts of Wales. Norman barons, the **Marcher Lords**, were installed in castles along the border so as to get control of as much land (and income) as possible. Welsh kings paid **homage** to the Normans, securing peace until William's death. William's son, William Rufus, made some incursions into Wales and the Marcher lords gradually helped to secure much of the country – although the northwest region of Gwynedd remained independent. There was much infighting and under **Owain Gwynedd**, operating from his power base at Aberffraw on Anglesey, Gwynedd began expanding its influence, sucking in weaker Welsh territories. **Llywelyn ap Iorwerth** (known as 'the Great') further extended Gwynedd and even managed to capture some Norman castles, until King John retaliated. Matters were complicated still more when Llywelyn, who wanted to achieve feudal overlordship over all Wales, consolidated his powerful position by marrying King John's daughter. He paid homage to the king and had to accept him as his heir, should his marriage not produce a son. Further struggles ensued, with Llywelyn gaining Welsh support for his demands for land and a degree of autonomy. He united with the barons who made King John sign the Magna Carta and, in essence, ruled most of Wales.

After he died, the infighting started again and the Normans pushed back into Wales until Llywelyn's grandson **Llywelyn ap Gruffyd** ('the Last') took control, managing to regain lost lands. In 1267 Henry III acknowledged his influence with the Treaty of Montgomery, in which Llywelyn recognized the English crown – and in turn was recognized as '**Prince of Wales**'. Llywelyn consolidated his lands, but then Edward I succeeded to the English throne and set out to gain control of the whole of Britain.

The Middle Ages and the last Welsh princes

Llywelyn gradually began to lose Welsh support and his brother Dafydd united against him with the ruler of Powys. Edward I seized his chance and the resulting struggle became known as the **First War of Welsh Independence** (1267-1277). The result was the **Treaty Of Aberconwy** (1277), in which Llywelyn lost most of his lands but was allowed to keep the title Prince of Wales. To keep the troublesome Welsh in order, Edward built castles at Flint, Aberystwyth, Builth Wells and Rhuddlan. A **Second War of Welsh Independence** was fought from 1282-1283, when Llywelyn's brother Dafydd rose against Edward, who brutally crushed the Welsh. Llywelyn was captured and killed at Cilmeri, near Builth Wells in 1282. Edward I strengthened his grip on Wales by starting to build more castles at Conwy, Caernarfon, Harlech and Beaumaris. In 1283 Dafydd was killed and the power of the Welsh princes ended.

In 1284 Edward signed the **Statute of Rhuddlan**, which established how Wales was to be governed; it was to be largely controlled by Norman lords and divided into new administrative units. English law took over for criminal matters, although Welsh law was retained for civil cases. Many of the powerful Welsh worked under this system happily enough and a rebellion in 1294 led by **Madog ap Llywelyn** was quickly crushed. In 1301 Edward revived the title of Prince of Wales, conferring it on his son Edward II, who had been born at Caernarfon.

The 14th century saw Britain plagued by famine and the Black Death, and Welsh anger and discontentment at their subjugation increased. The country was ripe for revolt – all

Arthur – the Once and Future King

With its ancient standing stones, prehistoric burial chambers, barren peaks and rich history it's not surprising that Wales is full of myths and legends, as well as tales of saints and holy wells, of giants and fairies, of Celtic gods and ghosts. And the best known figure of all is King Arthur.

The story of Arthur and the Knights of the Round Table is extraordinarily enduring and still inspires films and books. But did he exist? His name in Welsh, Arth Fawr, meaning the Great Bear, like the constellation Ursa Major, could point to him being a Celtic god. Some think the Arthurian legends date back to the Bronze Age, however, most sources feel he was probably a fifth-century Celtic chieftain who led the Brythonic Celts to victory against the Saxons. Though many places claim to be his birthplace, Tintagel in Cornwall seems the most likely, while Camelot could well be Cadbury Castle in Somerset. He is thought to have died at the battle of Camlan around AD 539 and his burial place is generally agreed to be Glastonbury. Nothing very Welsh there then, yet Arthur has featured in Welsh folklore for centuries.

The first written references to him were made in the ninth-century *Historia Brittonum*, written by Nennius a monk from Bangor. Artorius was the 'dux bellorum' the leader who defeated the Saxons at Badon Hill in AD 518. By the 12th century he was a powerful symbol and was mentioned in the *Black Book of Carmarthen*, the oldest Welsh manuscript; in the *Mabinogion*, the famed collection of Welsh folk tales; and in Geoffrey of Monmouth's mammoth *Historia Regum Britanniae* – a 12-volume history of the kings of Britain. Geoffrey essentially wrote the first Arthurian romance and claimed that Caerleon, near Newport, was the site of his first court; the mound covering the ruined Roman amphitheatre there was known for years as Arthur's Round Table.

Later, writers embellished the myth, gradually turning Arthur from a Celtic leader to an idealized courtly knight. Chrétien de Troyes, a French poet, took the story to France and in the 15th century Sir Thomas Mallory wrote his influential *Morte d'Arthur*.

Welsh versions of his story abound, claiming that he fought his last battle on Snowdon; that Llyn Llydaw, a lake at the foot of Snowdon, was where the dying king was rowed out to the island of Avalon; that Excalibur was thrown by Sir Bedivere into Llyn Ogwen (or Llyn Llydaw or the lily pond at Bosherston…); and that Merlin sank the crown jewels into Llyn Cwmglas, a lake above the Llanberis Pass. Avalon is sometimes thought to be Bardsey Island; and Camlan, the site of his last battle, could be Cadlan on the Llŷn Peninsula. Arthur, the Once and Future King, is still a powerful symbol of the Welsh struggle against oppression – a king who sleeps, waiting to come to the aid of the Celts once again.

they needed was a leader. In 1400, **Owain Glyndŵr** (1354-c1416) declared himself Prince of Wales and attacked ruling barons. He quickly gathered support and took castles such as Conwy, Harlech and Aberystwyth. Rebellion spread throughout Wales and Glyndŵr briefly established parliaments at Machynlleth and Dolgellau. He established alliances with powerful figures such as the Earl of Northumberland, and planned an independent Welsh state, garnering support from the Scots and the French. However, his support began to wane and after various defeats, with the Crown retaking Harlech and Aberystwyth castles he seemed to fade away. No one is sure how or when he died although it is thought to be 1416.

The Tudors

In 1485 Harri Tewdwr, a Welshman, took the English throne after winning the Battle of Bosworth with the help of a Welsh army. He became **Henry VII**, the first Tudor king, and Welsh hopes in him were high. He rewarded loyal Welsh nobles with high positions at court and sent letters to Welsh gentry in which he said he would restore 'the people… to their erst libertyes, delivering them of such miserable servitudes as they have pyteously longe stand in'. Restoration of 'libertyes' was not necessarily what Welsh nobles wanted – if interpreted in a certain way that could mean a return to the rigid traditional system of equal inheritance and the obstacles presented to the acquisition of land. They had seen at close hand the advantages of the English system of primogeniture and greater freedom in the transfer of land. The ruling class rapidly became anglicized.

Under Henry VIII's powerful administrator, Thomas Cromwell, Wales was brought far more under English control with the **Acts of Union** in 1536 and 1542. Although the Welsh were given legal equality, the legal system was unified with English common law taking the place of Welsh. The country was reorganized into shires, primogeniture became the method of inheritance and English became the language of the courts.

Elizabeth I

Under Elizabeth I, who wanted to ensure that Wales became Protestant rather than Catholic, an Act of Parliament was passed which laid down that the Bible be translated into Welsh within four years. This **Welsh Bible** should then be used in parishes where Welsh was the main language. The Welsh New Testament appeared in 1567, followed by the complete Bible in 1588. It was this that effectively saved the Welsh language. In 1547, the first Welsh book was published and, in 1571, Jesus College, Oxford was founded for Welsh scholars.

Civil War

During the Civil War, Wales was largely on the side of the king. Gradually Parliamentarian forces gained the upper hand but many castles resisted long sieges. **Harlech** was the last Royal castle to fall in 1647.

In 1752, Britain accepted the Gregorian Calendar. However, the Gwaun Valley in Pembrokeshire stayed with the Julian one – they still celebrate Julian New Year now.

Industrial Revolution

Wales was at the heart of the Industrial Revolution. While the north was rich in slate, the south was rich in iron ore, coal, limestone and water and the valleys around Merthyr Tydfil became huge centres for coal and iron production. Huge numbers of people migrated to the Valleys looking for work, and because many of them were not Welsh, local culture and language were weakened. The harsh conditions experienced by the workers gave rise to unrest throughout Britain. In Wales the **Merthyr Riots** of 1831 were particularly violent. The Red Flag was raised for the first time and many people, on both sides, were killed.

Insurrection continued with the **Chartist Riots**, the first of these in Wales took place in 1839 in Newport. The **Rebecca Riots** of 1839-1843 were a protest against toll gates on turnpike roads. They started on 13 May 1839 at Efail-wen. Rioters dressed in women's clothes and demolished the toll gates. The name was taken from a verse mentioning Rebecca in the Book of Genesis.

Welsh castles

The Welsh landscape is crammed with castles – brooding stone reminders of the country's turbulent history. There are 400 in all. But if you thought one was much like another you'd be wrong. Essentially there are three types of castle in Wales: those built by the Normans, those by the Welsh, and those by Edward I. They all have their own story to tell, and none more so than the handful of native Welsh castles that survive.

The first fortresses in Wales were erected by the Romans, whose imperial forces gradually subdued the ancient Britons who had retreated to this wild, western corner. However, castles, often built close to these Roman sites, did not appear until after the Norman Conquest and were erected by William's conquering forces to ensure that the locals knew just who was in charge. These were originally motte and bailey constructions of earth and timber, but later stone was used to create more robust structures. Most of the Norman castles in Wales are in the south and along the border with England. The first stone built castle in Britain was made by the Normans in Chepstow in 1067. It was the base for their aggressive incursions into Wales. Other Norman castles include Pembroke, Caerleon and Kidwelly.

In the 13th century, Welsh princes began to build their own castles, not just to provide protection against invading forces but also to guard against attacks from rival princes; this was a time when there were fierce internal struggles for control of Wales. These native Welsh castles were built in some of the most dramatic places in the country, utilising craggy outcrops and steep, isolated hills as natural defences. They tended to be smaller than Norman castles and often had a distinctive D-shaped tower. This had an outer, curved edge which gave a wide field of fire, and a flatter inner edge which meant that the rooms inside could be more spacious than in round towers. Only a few of these castles survive and they're often neglected by visitors. They include Castell-y-Bere, near Dolgellau, built to secure the southern border of Gwynedd; Dolbadarn, near Llanberis, and Dolwyddelan, south of Betws y Coed, which both guarded major routes through Snowdonia; and Dinefwr, in Carmarthenshire, which was the principal court of the kingdom of Deheubarth. Welsh castles fell into disrepair after the country was conquered by England, but the ruins are poignant and atmospheric reminders of the past.

The best known castles in Wales are those built by Edward I late in the 13th century. He was determined to complete the conquest of the Welsh, and as most danger came from North Wales, concentrated his building projects there. Some of his early castles were Rhuddlan and Conwy, and later Flint. But after Llywelyn the Last's second uprising he built even more enormous structures to create an iron ring of defence. These later castles of Harlech, Caernarfon, Conwy and finally Beaumaris remain among the most impressive and formidable castles in Europe. More information at www.castlewales.com.

Events such as the Rebecca Riots and the Chartist movement led many in authority to express concern at the increasingly negative attitude of the working classes. The issue of language, which was still being spoken in non-conformist schools, was thought to make the Welsh more prone to rioting. Welsh was also increasingly regarded as a handicap by parents, who saw it was important for their children to speak English so they could get on in industry and the professions. In 1846 a Welshman, representing an English constituency, set up an inquiry into Welsh education, focusing on the 'means afforded to the labouring classes of acquiring a knowledge of English'. English Anglicans were sent round the schools and came back with a report published in 1847. It declared that standards in education were terrible, which in many ways they were, but sadly they put much of this down to the use of Welsh. Their report was branded Brad y Llyfrau Gleision – the **'Treachery of the Blue Books'**. When free primary schools were set up in Wales in 1870, Welsh was largely banned. To dissuade pupils from speaking their language a 'Welsh Not' was introduced. This was a piece of wood on a strap which had to be worn, and was only passed on if someone else was heard speaking Welsh. The child left wearing the device would then be beaten.

In 1872 the system of education was expanded with the opening of the University College of Wales at Aberystwyth. A campaign began to grow for greater autonomy for Wales and there was a revival of interest in Welsh culture. The eisteddfod was reintroduced into Welsh life, the first being the National Eisteddfod of 1858. In 1885 the Welsh Language Society was created, which succeeded in ensuring that Welsh was taught in schools, and a political movement for a separate Wales was formed in 1886 as part of the Liberal party.

The political scene in Wales became increasingly radical and in 1900 Merthyr Tydfil elected a Scot, **Keir Hardie** as their MP – Britain's first Labour MP. The First World War saw a Welshman, **David Lloyd George** become prime Minister. The Labour Party continued to grow in importance in Wales, but there was dissatisfaction at their failure to introduce home rule for Wales and the lack of safeguards for the language. In 1925 **Plaid Cymru**, the National Party of Wales was established. One of the founders was Saunder Lewis. He and two other Plaid members – DJ Williams and Lewis Valentine – gained notoriety (and Welsh support) when they set fire to buildings at an RAF station on the Llŷn.

After the Second World War, Labour came to power and a Welsh MP **Aneurin Bevan** established the National Health Service. Wales was still at the heart of the coal mining industry; the Valleys were tragically brought to the world's attention in October 1966 when a slag heap slid down a hill engulfing a school in the close-knit mining village of **Aberfan**:144 people were killed, 116 of whom were children.

Nationalism and devolution

Over the years, demands for home rule increased again and in 1979 a **referendum** was held. The result was huge disappointment for the nationalists with 80% of people voting against a Welsh assembly. But interest in the Welsh language did increase (the 1967 Welsh Language Act had already allowed the use of Welsh in court) and in 1982 a Welsh-language television channel, **S4C**, started up. Nationalist protests began to be directed at English 'incomers' – particularly at those buying second homes in Wales. The Sons of Glyndŵr started setting fire to English-owned holiday homes, giving rise to the joke 'Come home to a real fire – buy a Welsh cottage'.

After the Thatcher government was finally defeated and Labour took power again, another referendum was held in 1997. This time there was a tiny majority in favour and elections to the **National Assembly for Wales** took place in May 1999. Unlike the Scottish Parliament it has no tax raising powers. After much wrangling work on a new building to house the assembly finally began in summer 2003. The Senedd, as it is known, was opened in 2006. It houses the National Assembly for Wales' Siambr (debating chamber) and Committee Rooms. The Assembly is made up of 60 Assembly Members – 40 representing individual constituencies and 20 representing the five regions of Wales. See www.assemblywales.org.

Culture

Literature

Myths and legends

The tradition of storytelling in Wales is rich and can be said to have its roots in the country's Celtic past. The Celts' religious system involved worship of gods, associated with natural features like flowers, trees and water. The Druids, the powerful religious and political Celtic leaders, had to undergo 20 years of training to acquire their sacred knowledge. This covered three areas: Druid – focusing on education and philosophy; Ovates – dealing with natural lore, divination and healing; and Bardic – the art of oratory – or powerful public speaking. Nothing was ever written down and everything had to be committed to memory. And with landscapes that inspire myths and legends (moody mountains, isolated islands, dank caves, ancient burial sites) there was plenty of material to inspire the early storytellers. And the battles fought both on and for the land, the arrival of the early Christian saints, and the colourful characters in Welsh history all added to this inspirational cocktail.

Many of the earliest stories survive in the *Mabinogion*, a rich collection of Welsh mythical tales written down around the 13th and 14th centuries but of much earlier origin. The *Mabinogion* were eventually translated into English in the 19th century by Lady Charlotte Guest, who gave them their collective title, which means 'Tales of Youth'. Characters who feature include Blodeuwedd, a girl who was created from flowers; and Culhwch, who has to perform forty feats to win the hand of Olwen, daughter of a local giant. He pulls it off with the help of King Arthur and his knights.

The Arthurian legends are rich in Wales. Not only do they appear in the Mabinogion but are also mentioned in the ninth century Historia Brittonum, a Latin history of Britain by Nennius who, according to what you read, was either a monk in Wales or a military leader from Scotland. Arthur is considered by many to have been a tribal leader who, much like Boudicca, fought off Saxon invaders. Merlin the magician, of the legends, is also said to be Welsh – probably a sixth-century holy man called Myrddin who was born near Carmarthen. Whether fact or fiction, Arthur certainly featured in an early Welsh poem, *Y Gododdin*; written around the seventh century by the bard Aneurin, it describes a battle against the Saxons.

Travel writing

Travel writers have also been intrigued by Wales' unique combination of ancient language, rich history and stunning scenery. The first was **Giraldus Cambrensis**, or Gerald of Wales, who was born at Manorbier in 1146. Of Norman descent, he travelled widely through Wales trying to drum up recruits to go on the Third Crusade, and wrote detailed accounts of his travels. The books, *The Journey Through Wales* and *The Description of Wales*, give a vivid insight into Welsh life and people in the 12th century. Other travel books include **Thomas Pennant's** A Tour in Wales (1773), which ushered in a passion for wild and romantic Welsh landscapes; **HV Morton's** In Search of Wales; and **George Borrow's** still widely quoted *Wild Wales* (1854). Borrow was English but had learned Welsh and reported his conversations in detail. He is often seen as typifying English condescending attitudes towards the Welsh – but as this is the man who wrote "an Englishman of the lower class ... is never savage with you, provided you call him old chap, and he considers you by your dress to be his superior in station" he was obviously happy to patronize anyone, not just the Welsh.

Poetry

Poetry has enormous importance in Wales, with Aneurin and Taliesin – a sixth-century bard associated with the poems that appeared in the 14th-century *Book of Taliesin* – providing the earliest examples of Welsh poetry. Poets were important members of the royal courts and Welsh princes had their own poets to record battles and important events – and praise their bosses, a bit like the Poet Laureate today. The earliest known of these professional bards was a man named Meilyr who lived in the 12th century. An intricate and characteristic form of poetry writing gradually developed at these courts. Known as *cynghanedd* – the use of vivid imagery and elaborate patterns of rhyme and alliteration – its influence can still be seen today.

Poetry was considered so important that competitions were established, with poets competing for privileged positions. The first recorded large scale competition – or eisteddfod – took place in 1176 at Rhys ap Gruffydd's castle in Cardigan. These flourished until the 17th and 18th centuries, when they began to peter out, until they were revived in the 19th century. Poetry had enormous significance for the Welsh, often mourning the loss of great leaders who had fought their English/Norman rulers, and stirring the emotions of a people who desperately wanted to be free.

19th- and 20th-century literature

After 1870 the speaking of English, rather than Welsh, was enforced in schools and a new Anglo/Welsh literature emerged, with Welsh people writing in English but being influenced by the Welsh writing traditions and patterns of speech. The country itself also acted as inspiration to poets. The Jesuit poet **Gerard Manley Hopkins** (1844-1889), writing in the 1870s and 1880s, was inspired and moved by the Welsh countryside as well as the rhythm of the language. And **Edward Thomas** (1878-1917) who was of Welsh extraction, produced fine poems inspired by nature until he was killed at the Front in the First World War. **WH Davies** (1871-1940), a friend of Thomas, left Wales for America, where his experiences on the road inspired the once bestselling, but now less widely read, *Autobiography of a Super-Tramp*. However his lines "What is this life if, full of care/We have no time to stand and stare" have entered the British lexicon.

The 20th century saw the real flowering of Welsh writing – and not only were Welsh people writing in English, Wales itself was inspiring literature. **Caradoc Evans** (1914-1945) wrote controversial and satirical works about non-conformist Wales; novelist **Richard Hughes** (1900-1976), author of *High Wind in Jamaica*, lived and worked in Laugharne; **Alexander Cordell** (1914-1997) settled in Wales and wrote novels inspired by Welsh historical events such as the Rebecca Riots; **Kingsley Amis** (1922-1995) lectured at Swansea University – the setting for his novel *Lucky Jim* (1954), and Welshman **Alun Lewis** (1915-1944) produced some of the most important poetry of the Second World War. The book that really grabbed popular attention was **Richard Llewellyn**'s *How Green Was My Valley* (1939), a worldwide bestseller depicting life in the coalfields of south Wales – which later got the Hollywood treatment in a film.

The most acclaimed 20th-century writers were poets RS Thomas and Dylan Thomas. **RS Thomas** (1913-2000) was a clergyman and prolific writer who was inspired by the landscapes and history of Wales. His work had a bleak quality "There is no present in Wales/ And no future;/ There is only the past." He was a fierce nationalist too and spoke out on issues such as the spread of the English language into isolated, mainly Welsh-speaking areas. **Dylan Thomas** (1914-1953) is the best known of all Welsh writers, not only because of the high quality of his rich, original and lyrical verse, but also because of his reputation for hard living and hard drinking. Born in Swansea, his first volume of work was *Eighteen Poems* which was received to widespread acclaim. Over the years he moved to London and then back to Wales, producing fine poems with instantly recognizable lines such as: "Do not go gentle into that good night" and "The force that through the green fuse". He also wrote the dense and compelling *Under Milk Wood*, his 'play for voices', which produced characters such as Captain Cat and Polly Garter. When he wasn't writing poetry he was investigating the pubs of southwest Wales. His heavy drinking leading to his untimely death in America, where a particularly hard session resulted in "an insult to the brain".

Literature today

Literature is flourishing in Wales today and it is worth looking for works by poets such as **Menna Elfyn**, **Owen Sheers** and **Harri Webb**; Welsh romantic novels by the prolific **Iris Gower**, and works by **Kate Roberts** set in the quarries of north Wales. Then there's the Welsh Irvine Welsh, **Niall Griffiths**, whose books like *Grits* and *Sheepshagger* look at the seamy side of contemporary life; **James Hawes**, whose *White Powder*, *Green Light*, focuses on the Welsh media; and **Malcolm Pryce's** blackly comic *Aberystwyth Mon Amour*.

Music

Wales and Music – a musical tradition

The epithet 'land of song' has been attached to Wales since Adam was a lad. And, true enough, the country has a powerful musical tradition. Its male voice choirs are known throughout the world, and top-flight artists such as Tom Jones and Shirley Bassey are household names. The Welsh National Opera has performed in the world's foremost venues. When virtuoso Bryn Terfel appeared at the Metropolitan Opera in 1998, he made the front page of the *New York Times*, and hot mezzo soprano Katherine Jenkins has a huge following. But these are conventional examples of the nation's culture – there's a lot more in the musical melting pot than this. Wales has an eclectic attitude to music, revelling in its many facets. Organizations such as Cultural Concerns bring musicians from around the globe: Burundi, Iran, Zimbabwe, India, Poland, Colombia to name a few, to perform in Wales. Likewise, Welsh artists take the opportunity to explore cultural differences and indeed similarities, in far-flung corners of the globe. And as for rock and pop, Wales produced The Manic Street Preachers, Stereophonics, Catatonia, Feeder, Super Furry Animals and Gorky's Zygotic Mynci, a pretty illustrious track record if ever there was one.

But why Wales and song? Why do the lusty voices of the rugby crowd belt out 'Calon Lan' and 'Sosban Fach' while the match is in full flood? What drives thousands of people to a free concert given by Welsh National Opera in Cardiff Bay? Why do pubs throughout the land reverberate to the sound, not only of the jukebox, but of imbibers boisterously accompanying their favourite number? And this isn't just drunken crooning, it actually sounds melodic!

Music, and song, is, and always has been, a compelling form of self-expression. Furthermore, Celtic societies, be they Breton, Cornish, Irish, Scottish or Welsh, have always cherished music. Music affirms an individual's sense of place and belonging. Traditional Welsh music explores the universal themes of love and desire, but it also explores the condition of *hiraeth*. No single word sums up this emotion, a sense of loss and longing and nostalgia. Expats express a sense of *hiraeth* when they think of home. But *hiraeth* is more than homesickness, it's part of the human condition, an inexpressible yearning. Inexpressible, that is, other than through music and song. Although the Welsh do a fine line in poetry and prose, the voice of the nation is most eloquently and profoundly expressed through the medium of music.

The earliest recorded instrument in Wales is the **crwth**, or lyre. There's evidence to suggest that it was played as far back as Roman times. This rudimentary instrument wasn't peculiar to the Celts though. An illustration on an Egyptian tomb circa 1900 BC shows a musician holding a six-stringed instrument that is, to all intents and purposes, a crwth. Its heyday came in the Middle Ages when players made a good living entertaining the Welsh aristocracy. Its popularity declined with the advent of the fiddle, with its infinitely more dexterous repertoire. Now, originals can be found at the Museum of Welsh Life in St Fagan's near Cardiff and in the National Library of Wales in Aberystwyth. However, the age of the crwth isn't completely over. Enthusiasts, such as widely acclaimed fiddle player Cass Meurig, still perform traditional crwth music and replicas are lovingly fashioned by Cardiff-based craftsman, Guy Flockhart.

Bagpipes may be synonymous with Scotland, but all Celtic nations have their own version. The Welsh manifestation is called the 'piba cwd'. Popular until the latter half of the nineteenth century, it is extraordinary that no examples have survived to the present day. Another popular instrument was the **pibgorn**, literally meaning hornpipe, which was not unique to Wales. This simple instrument is powered by a single reed like the drone reed of a bagpipe.

The **triple harp**, with its sweetly lyrical sound, is another instrument closely aligned with Wales. Unlike the crwth it has a prominent place in today's culture. Prince Charles revived an ancient tradition when he appointed 20-year-old Catrin Finch as Royal Harpist. The young Welshwoman's mission is to bring the harp to the masses. With her youth and good looks, she has a better chance of success than most of making the harp hip.

The Welsh **male voice choir** (cor meibion) is something of an institution. Although male choirs are found throughout the nation, they are perhaps most closely associated with the mining communities in South Wales. The demise of the coal industry isn't reflected in the fate of the choirs, joining one might not be a funky move, but the tradition still holds firm.

Classical music enjoys a high profile in Wales. Cardiff hosts the acclaimed *Singer of the World* competition, attended by the great and the good among classical vocalists, on an annual basis. **Welsh National Opera** (WNO) is recognized as one of the UK's finest companies, and was the first ever regional company to appear at Covent Garden. The performing arts are devotedly nurtured at the Welsh College of Music and Drama and within the BBC's National Orchestra of Wales.

The **Manic Street Preachers** paved the way for Wales to become a feature on the rock'n'roll map. Catatonia's **Cerys Matthews**, raunchy and vivid, coined the immortal words 'Everyday I wake up, and thank the lord I'm Welsh.' For a brief and wonderful moment, the South Wales city Newport was hailed as the new Seattle. For those jaded with the 'We'll Keep A Welcome in the Hillsides' image of Wales, this feisty new face represented a freedom from the shackles of tradition. For the first time ever it was cool to be Welsh. The term 'Cool Cymru' or 'Cool Wales' entered the lexicon.

Rhondda, the most famous of all the South Wales mining valleys, struck out into new waters with a musical venture called **The Factory** (formerly The Pop Factory) ① *T02920-230130, www.factoryporth.com*. This sleek venue and television complex has worked hard to attract big names, with notable success.

Despite the success of Welsh bands, some would say that the contemporary music scene has stalled. At least, in terms of bands big enough to hit the headlines and stay there. However, all is not lost. The Welsh Music Foundation has been set up to nurture modern Welsh music, and maximize its cultural and economic potential. Sadly, to date, the mother country has benefited very little in monetary terms from the success of its high-flying sons and daughters. In future that should change, and Wales can reap financial and emotional rewards from her aeons-long love affair with music.

Welsh language

Welsh origins

Welsh is an Indo-European language presumably descended like many languages in modern Western Europe from languages that were originally spoken on the steppes of Central Asia. It is immediately descended from the Brythonic language, its closest relatives are other Celtic languages – Cornish and Breton. To the present day there remain differences in dialects throughout Wales, the most notable being: Y Wyndodeg (northwest), Y Buwyseg (northeast and mid Wales), Y Ddyfydeg (southwest), Gwenhwyseg (southeast).

During the dark ages, Wales was ruled by a number of different Welsh dynastic principalities who from time to time made alliances with each other and English rulers. It was during this time that the Brythonic language was consolidated and became widespread throughout Wales. It was influenced to a degree by the Roman occupation, and even today, the Welsh language shows Latin influences with words like *pont* (bridge), *ffenestre* (window), *caws* (cheese) and *cwmwl* (cloud).

In the 15th century, Wales was absorbed into the English state under Henry VIII. This was the first reference to the Welsh language. The passing of the 1536 and 1542 Acts of Union brought significant change as it stated that English should be the only language in courts. Use of the Welsh language, in an official capacity, was not lawful again until the passing of the Welsh Courts Act in 1942.

On the request of Elizabeth I, the Bible was translated by William Morgan in 1588, establishing a nationwide standard for the language. Welsh was permitted as the language of religion and church, helping to safeguard it. Had this not been the case the language could have disappeared completely at this stage.

In 1847, the 'Report of the Commissioners of Inquiry Into the State of Education in Wales', written by three English commissioners, emphasized the superiority of the English language. The 'Welsh not' or 'Welsh stick' was introduced in some schools – a form of punishment handed out to pupils found speaking Welsh, which could result in a beating. This practice became a symbol of oppression of the language.

The establishment of 'Yr Eisteddfod Genedlaethol' in the 19th century and the importance of the Welsh chapel, frequently the centre of Welsh life, were important in keeping the grass-roots language alive. By 1911, nearly a million people regarded themselves as Welsh speakers. However, social change such as urbanization, industrialization and the secularization of society, led to English becoming the main language (50%) in some areas.

National Eisteddfod

The National Eisteddfod, an annual cultural festival and competition to celebrate Welsh culture, is now a vital part of the Welsh calendar. In 1938, a petition was launched at the Eisteddfod calling for a repeal of the Act of Union, demanding that Welsh be given equal status with English. The petition, signed by more than a quarter of a million people and supported by a number of Welsh MPs, led to the Welsh Courts Act of 1942. The Welsh language became legally acceptable in schools, for academic studies and the media; however, the language clause of the Act of Union remained, which held sway in the courts of law.

Welsh National Party

Plaid Genedlaethol Cymru (The Welsh National Party) was formed in Pwllheli in 1925 by a small group of intellectuals and their leader, Saunders Lewis, focused the party efforts on the defence of the Welsh language. Cymdeithas yr Iaith was established in 1962 as one of the first single issue pressure groups. Using a non-violent means of civil disobedience, it led a campaign towards the Welsh Language Act 1967, which made the existence of Welsh language a more accepted part of life in the principality. It is predominately due to Cymdeithas yr Iaith that you will see bilingual road signs, as this was brought about in the 1960s when they launched a large-scale campaign against monolingual road signs.

The activities of Cymdeithas yr Iaith coincided with the granting to Wales of a significant degree of administrative autonomy by the appointment of a Minister of State for Wales in 1964 and the establishment of the Welsh Office.

Education and media

In 1988 the Education Reform Act ensured that all children aged between 5-16 would be taught Welsh as a core subject in Welsh medium schools. The growth in Welsh-medium education in places such as Cardiff produced considerable numbers of Welsh speakers and helped vary the social base of the language. The growth of Welsh in Anglicized districts was particularly evident in the results of the 1991 census.

Sianel Pedwar Cymru (S4C– Welsh Channel Four) was first broadcast in November 1982. This channel produces Welsh language programmes with English subtitles and a number of S4C's programmes are viewed across Europe. In the early 1980s when other sectors of the Welsh economy were in decline, there was significant rise in employment in Welsh language television. Welsh, in all aspects of life, has been given a higher status, particularly since the launch of the 1993 Welsh Language Act.

Devolution

In 1997 the devolution referendum was seen as an opportunity for greater autonomy for Wales and was supported as a means to reassert the 'Welsh' identity. The economic benefits of the Welsh language are being recognized, leading to the ability to communicate in Welsh and English in the workplace being recognized as a valuable skill and marketable commodity. The 2001 census identified the first increase in number and percentage of Welsh speakers in 20 counties, with the southeast showing the greatest rise. The language is evolving and gradually English phrases are being absorbed into the Welsh language.

Despite the turbulent times the language has experienced, its increased usage in all sectors of Welsh society has ensured a place in the hearts of the growing proportion of the population who chose to learn or pass on knowledge of the language. Welsh, one of the oldest European languages, is now spoken by almost a quarter of the population of Wales and a visitor is sure to see unusual phrases and hear unfamiliar sounds, but this is part of Wales' charm. Try and get your tongue around some basic 'Welsh' and you'll receive a warm welcome wherever you go.

Contents

Footnotes

Useful words and phrases

Alphabet (Yr Wyddor)
a, b, c, ch, d, dd, e, f, ff, g, ng, h, i, i, i, l, ll, m, n, o, p, ph, r, rh, s, t, th, u, w, y

Vowels (llafariad)
a, e, i, o, u, w, y

A aah	B bee	C eck	CH ech
D dee	DD edd	E air	F ev
FF eff	G egg	NG eng	H high-tsh
I ee	J jay	L el	LL ell
M em	N en	O oh	P pee
PH phee	R air	RH air-hee	S ess
T tee	TH eth	U ee	W oo Y uh

Welsh place names	Meaning	Pronunciation
Abertawe (Swansea)	Estuary	Ab-er-taw-eh
Beddgelert	Grave	Be-the-gel-airt
Betws-y-**Coed**	Wood	Bet-oos uh koyd
Caerdydd (Cardiff)	Fort	K-ie-r-dee-the
Cas**newydd** (Newport)	New	Kas ne with
Dinbych-y-**Pysgod** (Denbigh)	Fish	Din-bich uh pusg-od
Glan **Llyn**	Lake	Glan ll-in
Llandeilo	Church	ll-an-day-lo
Sir Benfro (Pembrokeshire)	County	Seer Ben Vr-aw
Y **Dre**newydd (Newtown)	Town	Uh Drair ne with
Ynys Mon (Anglesey)	Island	Un- is Morn

Llanfairpwllgwyngyllgogerychwyrndrobwllllantysiliogogogoch

Roughly translated as:
The Church of St Mary by the pool with the white hazel near the rapid whirlpool by St Tysilio's church and the red cave.

Have a go at pronouncing it:
Thlann vyre pooth gwin gith gogger ich chweern drobbooth lann tuss-illyo goggo gauch.

Other useful phrases:

Bore Da	good morning	*Prynhawn da*	good afternoon
Nos da	good night	*Hwyl fawr*	good bye
Diolch	thank you	*Dim diolch*	no thank you
Os gwelwch chi'n dda	please	*Faint?*	how much?
Gwely a brecwast	bed and breakfast	*Lwc dda*	Good luck
Paned o de	cup of tea	*Paned o goffi*	cup of coffee

Glossary

A
Afon – river
Amgueddfa – museum
Ap (ab) – son of
Ar Agor – open
Ar Gau – closed

B
Bach – small
Bara – bread
Blaen – head of valley
Brenhines – queen
Brenin – king
Bryn – hill
Bwlch – pass
Brecwast – breakfast
Bws – bus

C
Cadair – chair, stronghold
Capel – chapel
Carn – rock, mountain
Carreg – rock, stone
Castell – castle
Cefn – ridge
Clun – meadow
Coch – red
Croeso – welcome
Cwm – valley (or combe)
Cymraeg – Welsh
Cymru – Wales
Cymry – the Welsh people

D
Da – good
Ddu / Du – black
De – south
Dinas – town, fort
Dŵr – water
Dwyrain – east
Dydd – day

E
Eglwys – church

F
Fawr – big
Fferm – farm
Ffordd – road, way
Fforest – forest
Ffynnon – well

G
Glan – river bank
Gardd – garden
Glas – blue
Glyn – vallley, glen
Gogledd – north
Gorllewin – west
Gorsaf – station
Gwely – bed
Gwesty – hotel
Gwyn – white
Gwyrdd – green

H
Hafod – summer dwelling
 for herdsmen
Heddiw – today
Hen – old
Heol – road
Hiraeth – yearning

I
Isaf – lower

L
Llechen – slate
Llety – lodging
Llwybr – path
Llys – court

M
Maen – rock, stone
Maes – field
Mawr – big, great
Melin – mill
Melyn – yellow
Merthyr – martyr
Môr – sea
Morfa – marsh
Mynydd – mountain

N
Nant – stream
Neuadd – hall
Newydd – new
Nos – night

O
Ogof – cave

P
Pant – dip
Parc – park
Pen – head of
Pentre/pentref – village
Plas – hall (large house)
Pont (bont) – bridge
Porth – port or doorway

R
Rhaeadr – waterfall
Rhiw – hill

S
Saesneg – English (language)
Sarn – causeway
Sant – saint
Siop – shop
Stryd – street
Swyddfa'r Post – post office

T
Tafarn – pub
Theatr – theatre
Traeth – beach
Tre, tref – town
Tŵr – tower
Tŷ – house

U
Uchaf – highest

Y
Y, Yr, 'r' – the
Yn – in
Ysbyty – hospital
Ysgol – school

Index

Titles available in the Footprint *Focus* range

Latin America	UK RRP	US RRP
Bahia & Salvador	£7.99	$11.95
Brazilian Amazon	£7.99	$11.95
Brazilian Pantanal	£6.99	$9.95
Buenos Aires & Pampas	£7.99	$11.95
Cartagena & Caribbean Coast	£7.99	$11.95
Costa Rica	£8.99	$12.95
Cuzco, La Paz & Lake Titicaca	£8.99	$12.95
El Salvador	£5.99	$8.95
Guadalajara & Pacific Coast	£6.99	$9.95
Guatemala	£8.99	$12.95
Guyana, Guyane & Suriname	£5.99	$8.95
Havana	£6.99	$9.95
Honduras	£7.99	$11.95
Nicaragua	£7.99	$11.95
Northeast Argentina & Uruguay	£8.99	$12.95
Paraguay	£5.99	$8.95
Quito & Galápagos Islands	£7.99	$11.95
Recife & Northeast Brazil	£7.99	$11.95
Rio de Janeiro	£8.99	$12.95
São Paulo	£5.99	$8.95
Uruguay	£6.99	$9.95
Venezuela	£8.99	$12.95
Yucatán Peninsula	£6.99	$9.95

Asia	UK RRP	US RRP
Angkor Wat	£5.99	$8.95
Bali & Lombok	£8.99	$12.95
Chennai & Tamil Nadu	£8.99	$12.95
Chiang Mai & Northern Thailand	£7.99	$11.95
Goa	£6.99	$9.95
Gulf of Thailand	£8.99	$12.95
Hanoi & Northern Vietnam	£8.99	$12.95
Ho Chi Minh City & Mekong Delta	£7.99	$11.95
Java	£7.99	$11.95
Kerala	£7.99	$11.95
Kolkata & West Bengal	£5.99	$8.95
Mumbai & Gujarat	£8.99	$12.95

Africa & Middle East	UK RRP	US RRP
Beirut	£6.99	$9.95
Cairo & Nile Delta	£8.99	$12.95
Damascus	£5.99	$8.95
Durban & KwaZulu Natal	£8.99	$12.95
Fès & Northern Morocco	£8.99	$12.95
Jerusalem	£8.99	$12.95
Johannesburg & Kruger National Park	£7.99	$11.95
Kenya's Beaches	£8.99	$12.95
Kilimanjaro & Northern Tanzania	£8.99	$12.95
Luxor to Aswan	£8.99	$12.95
Nairobi & Rift Valley	£7.99	$11.95
Red Sea & Sinai	£7.99	$11.95
Zanzibar & Pemba	£7.99	$11.95

Europe	UK RRP	US RRP
Bilbao & Basque Region	£6.99	$9.95
Brittany West Coast	£7.99	$11.95
Cádiz & Costa de la Luz	£6.99	$9.95
Granada & Sierra Nevada	£6.99	$9.95
Languedoc: Carcassonne to Montpellier	£7.99	$11.95
Málaga	£5.99	$8.95
Marseille & Western Provence	£7.99	$11.95
Orkney & Shetland Islands	£5.99	$8.95
Santander & Picos de Europa	£7.99	$11.95
Sardinia: Alghero & the North	£7.99	$11.95
Sardinia: Cagliari & the South	£7.99	$11.95
Seville	£5.99	$8.95
Sicily: Palermo & the Northwest	£7.99	$11.95
Sicily: Catania & the Southeast	£7.99	$11.95
Siena & Southern Tuscany	£7.99	$11.95
Sorrento, Capri & Amalfi Coast	£6.99	$9.95
Skye & Outer Hebrides	£6.99	$9.95
Verona & Lake Garda	£7.99	$11.95

North America	UK RRP	US RRP
Vancouver & Rockies	£8.99	$12.95

Australasia	UK RRP	US RRP
Brisbane & Queensland	£8.99	$12.95
Perth	£7.99	$11.95

For the latest books, e-books and a wealth of travel information, visit us at:
www.footprinttravelguides.com.

footprinttravelguides.com

Join us on facebook for the latest travel news, product releases, offers and amazing competitions:
www.facebook.com/footprintbooks.